Free-Motion Quilting
for Beginners

Free-Motion Quilting
for Beginners
and those who think they can't

Techniques, Designs, and Projects
for Your Home Sewing Machine

Molly Hanson

Martingale
Create with Confidence

Free-Motion Quilting for Beginners:
And Those Who Think They Can't
© 2014 by Molly Hanson

Martingale®
19021 120th Ave. NE, Ste. 102
Bothell, WA 98011-9511 USA
ShopMartingale.com

Printed in China
19 18 17 16 15 14   8 7 6 5 4 3 2 1

Library of Congress Cataloging-in-Publication Data
is available upon request.

ISBN: 978-1-60468-471-1

Dedication

To two people without whose help this book would
not have been possible:

My lovely grandmother and friend, Patricia Ditter,
whose experience, enthusiasm, and willingness to
test and help write my patterns were absolutely
indispensable. Rarely does a woman in her
thirties get to collaborate on a project with her
grandmother in her eighties. For this rare and
special experience, I will forever be grateful. Thank
you, Grandma. Your belief in me is the wind in
my sails.

My partner of over a decade, Jeff Armstrong. He
encouraged me to try quilting when I needed
an artistic outlet and a way to love my nieces
and nephews from afar. From picking fabrics to
researching quality machine needles or helping out
in a crisis, he is always willing to roll up his sleeves
and jump in with both feet. He always believed I
could do something with my quilting, and I am so
very lucky to have him. Thank you, Jeff. I love you.

Mission Statement

Dedicated to providing quality products and service
to inspire creativity.

Credits

PUBLISHER AND CHIEF VISIONARY OFFICER:
    Jennifer Erbe Keltner
EDITOR IN CHIEF: Mary V. Green
DESIGN DIRECTOR: Paula Schlosser
MANAGING EDITOR: Karen Costello Soltys
ACQUISITIONS EDITOR: Karen M. Burns
TECHNICAL EDITOR: Nancy Mahoney
COPY EDITOR: Melissa Bryan
PRODUCTION MANAGER: Regina Girard
COVER AND INTERIOR DESIGNER: Connor Chin
PHOTOGRAPHER: Brent Kane
ILLUSTRATORS: Lisa Lauch and Rose Wright

Contents

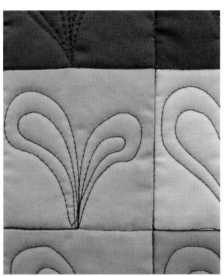

Foreword

Machine quilting is the most fun part of making a quilt, at least in my opinion. But as much as I love to machine quilt, I'm just as passionate about teaching others how to quilt. I think that anyone can learn and hone their machine-quilting skills, regardless of their experience or machine. That's why I am so excited about Molly's new book. Aimed at the beginning machine quilter, she is proving that you don't need a long-arm machine to be great at machine quilting!

I have the pleasure of calling Molly my friend. She is talented, spunky, and so personable, and her writing style reflects her personality perfectly. In this book, readers will be able to go on a journey, with Molly by their side, creating fun projects and learning how to machine quilt. With practical tips and her knowledge, I know they won't be disappointed.

~ **Angela Walters**
Machine quilter, author, friend

Introduction

I came to this hobby of quilting from humble beginnings. My childhood was a modest one, with loving and creative parents who celebrated the arts and never made my brother, sister, and me feel like we should judge ourselves by the standards of society. My parents also taught us to make do with what we had, to be clever about solving problems, and to teach ourselves what we wanted to learn. I brought this can-do attitude to my young-adult life, and when nieces and nephews started arriving, I felt a deep need to give those babies heirloom gifts. I felt handmade was the best, so I decided to teach myself to make a quilt. Not having a lot of money or resources, I went to a big-box retailer, bought some fabric and an inexpensive sewing machine, and went on my way. I wasn't scared by the fact that I had never taken a lesson and had no idea what I was doing—I just did it. I opened the sewing-machine manual and read it cover to cover. I cut some squares and sewed them together. I'm not saying my first efforts were fine art, but I learned and grew and kept at it and got better.

When I was approached to write this book, one of the biggest questions that burned in my mind was, what would my *message* be? Sure

I can teach people how to free-motion quilt, and sure I can show people how to make cool things out of quilted pieces of fabric that they practiced free-motion quilting on, but what did I want people to take away from this book beyond some good tips and fun patterns? Surely there had to be a bigger point than just covering the basic beginner skills. After thinking about it for a week, it struck me, and I had my message—all thanks to my three-year-old niece, Ruby. Who would have thought? My darling niece asked me to read her a story. I agreed, but since we'd already read her most-requested story several times, I insisted that this time *I* would choose the book. I thumbed through her bookshelf until an interesting title and cover caught my eye. It was a book called *The Dot* by Peter H. Reynolds (Candlewick Press, 2003). I don't have children of my own, but I'm sure many of you do and you may have read this story before. For those of you who aren't familiar with it, it's the tale of a little girl who doesn't think she is an artist, and therefore decides it would be best not to even try to draw. Her art teacher gently coaxes her into drawing a single dot on paper, and then asks that she sign her name. That single act inspires confidence and leads the girl to share her confidence with others, inspiring them to try new things too. Just signing her name, that was all it took.

I think we can all relate to that story on some level. Maybe you don't feel like a free-motion quilter, so you're too scared to try. But staring at a blank sheet of paper (figuratively) and doubting yourself won't get you anywhere. Learning anything new can be a bit scary, but the results are always worth the effort. When you know how to quilt a project yourself, you retain artistic control from start to finish, and you can turn your quilting vision into reality—with practice, of course.

This leads me to my next point, that practice is essential to learning this skill. Muscle memory takes over when you practice a lot. Your muscles know just what to do to create the design, and thus your brain is free to think about how best to use the design artistically. Muscle memory is something that can only come from repetition—you cannot avoid the hours you must spend quilting to become a good free-motion quilter.

You can, however, avoid waste and getting stuck in a very common rut for new free-motion quilters, which is making practice squares. I encourage you *not* to spend too much time on practice squares. I know it's scary to piece

something beautiful and risk ruining it with quilting that is less than perfect. But if you want to become good at quilting, you'll need to get over that mentality. When you only work on practice squares, you limit your experience to a perfectly controlled situation. Imagine learning to drive by never leaving a parking lot. You may know how to park like a pro, but there are a lot of driving scenarios you'll never experience unless you're on the open road. Likewise, you need to quilt actual projects from the beginning.

For each type of quilting design included in this book, I have provided a "quilting map" to reinforce the quilt design, and I encourage you to try quilting the projects as I have. In the quilting map, the quilting designs are drawn in the appropriate areas, along with instructions about what to quilt first, where to stitch in the ditch, and anything else to be mindful of. As you quilt the projects in this book, be content with less-than-perfect quilting and don't use your best fabric. Allow yourself some room to fail and learn from it. It's OK. You're likely the only one who will ever notice your mistakes—and your first piecing probably was not perfect either. (I know mine wasn't!) So relax and have fun. I recommend good music and a relaxed attitude for free-motion quilting. Take a deep breath, stretch those shoulders and arms, put on your favorite album, and let's get started.

Tools

When it comes to tools for sewing, I confess to being a total minimalist. I don't like to fuss with a lot of gadgets, and I don't feel I need the latest, greatest products. I stick to the basics and only purchase tools, rulers, or templates that serve more than one purpose, or that are absolutely essential for a job I need them to do. I take this same approach when it comes to supplies for free-motion quilting. Below, you'll find a list of what I consider to be the essential tools for free-motion quilting, followed by a list of helpful tools (and there is a difference). Please look into the helpful ones and sample them if you like. As for the essentials, these are all required, so make sure to get them before going any further in this book.

ESSENTIAL TOOLS

Darning foot. An open- or closed-toe darning foot is a must. You can buy universal ones to fit your machine in a multitude of styles. I prefer an open-toe metal darning foot. If you decide to use a plastic one, I recommend doing a little online research, because there are great articles on the Internet about how to modify the plastic darning foot for improved performance and visibility.

Cleaned and oiled sewing machine, including the owner's manual. It's important to know how to properly clean and oil your sewing machine before learning free-motion quilting. Long hours of stitching can be hard on your machine, and proper maintenance is essential to keep your machine working smoothly. You'll be running lots and lots of thread through your machine and running the surface of the quilt over the needle plate for hours at a time. The lint buildup will be something you have likely never seen before. You need to learn to deal with this properly. I suggest consulting your sewing-machine manual and reading up on cleaning and oiling your machine. **Note:** Some newer machines don't require oil and don't come apart fully for cleaning. This will limit the life of the machine, and free-motion quilting can hasten that process. Keep your machine as clean as you can by removing lint from all areas you can access.

Quilting extension table or drop-in sewing table. You'll need a flat surface area in order to keep your hands in the proper position as you move your project during quilting. At the very least, it's essential that you have an extension table for your machine. For more on this, see "Setting Up Your Space" on page 11.

Tools for free-motion quilting

High-quality quilting needles. I like 90/14 or 80/12 Schmetz or Organ topstitching needles, although Klassé needles are good too. I also love needles made from titanium, because they are extremely strong. My favorite brand of titanium needles is Organ. They are more expensive, but I buy them when I can, because they really do last longer. And since free-motion quilting puts more stress on your needle than piecing, needle quality and strength are important. It's a good idea to start each quilting project with a new needle, and when quilting large quilts, remember to change the needle occasionally—especially if you can hear the needle punching through the fabric.

Sketchbook and fine-point marker. The act of drawing designs is essential for the muscle memory and spatial planning involved in free-motion quilting. These tools will be discussed further in "Sketching" on page 19, but I assure you, they are all essential!

HELPFUL TOOLS

Quilting gloves. These gloves have a grippy texture designed to help you move the quilt around under the needle easily. Statistically, you will probably like quilting with these gloves—95% of quilters I talk to swear by them. I'm in the 5% of quilters who feel restricted by them; I just don't like the feeling of things on my hands. Since so many quilters find them helpful, I recommend that you give them a try and decide for yourself.

Supreme Slider. This is a very slick-surfaced mat that goes over your quilting extension table and allows the quilt to glide more freely. I like mine, but I don't *need* it. Sometimes I use it, and just as often I don't. Many quilters won't quilt without one. I do feel that purchasing one is worthwhile, especially if you'll be quilting a larger quilt. Anything that helps you move larger quilts more easily is worth owning.

Supreme Slider

Setting Up Your Space

Having the proper setup for free-motion quilting will aid you in your quilting progress more than any tool, tip, or trick. It will allow you the space to freely move your project, so you're able to focus on creating beautiful designs. A proper setup will also save your back and shoulders, and potentially your wrists and hands, from a lot of aching. I don't want to hear any groaning from you youngsters on this point. I began quilting when I was in my very early thirties, not a typical age for aches and pains. When I began, I didn't have a good setup, and I paid for it with plenty of soreness. So do yourself a favor and pay attention to the following information. Your body will thank you!

When planning your space for free-motion quilting, there are two major priorities: having enough space to move the quilt freely to create your designs and positioning your chair at the proper height.

ROOM TO MOVE

When you free-motion quilt, you want to position your hands so your thumbs are touching and are in front of your needle, and your hands are extended straight on either side of the needle, palms and fingertips flat. In that position you have a nice area to work in and it's easy to reposition your hands when necessary. This allows you the control to keep things nice and taut under your fingers, and you can use the full weight of your hands to help you grip the quilt. This is really important; if you don't have room for your palms to lie flat, then you don't have enough space. Most machines come with an extension table (shown below)—this is a minimum space requirement for free-motion quilt-ing on a domestic machine. The extension table will typically give you enough room to move your hands freely.

As an alternative, you could look into a sewing table where your machine drops in and the surface of the machine bed is level with the table. This type of setup (shown on page 12) is ideal for free-motion quilting, and it's what I use myself. Tables like this can be costly, and there are many factors to consider before investing in one. After much research, my guy Jeff and I decided it would be better to custom build one than to buy one. For us it was more cost effective and allowed the customization I desired. If you're considering that option, you can read on my blog about how Jeff put my table together. On my blog home page, SewWrongSewRight.blogspot.com, type *sewing table* into the "Search This Blog" field at the bottom of the page.

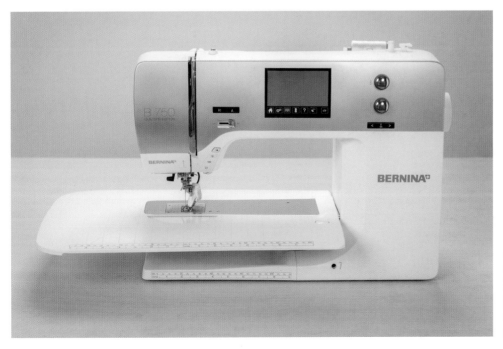

Almost every machine either comes with or has as an option to purchase some sort of extension table like the one shown here.

With a drop-in sewing table, the machine bed is level with the table surface, essentially turning your table into a giant extension table. This is an ideal setup for free-motion quilting.

SITTING PRETTY

The second priority in your setup is positioning your chair at the right height. Your elbows should make a perfect 90° angle when your forearms and palms are flat on your sewing surface. Your shoulders should be relaxed. Have a friend look at you and evaluate. If your elbows aren't at 90°, then you'll become sore when quilting, which is easily avoidable. If you don't already have an adjustable-height office chair, it's worth purchasing one if you'll be doing much quilting. With an adjustable height, you can position the chair just right so you're as comfortable as possible.

Once your elbows are at the right angle, you need to consider your right foot and the sewing pedal. If your feet aren't flat on the floor, you won't be comfortable for long. You want to be able to control your quilting speed just like you control your speed while driving. It's important to have your foot flat

Raise the Pedal

If you have trouble reaching the foot pedal (you're probably short like me), hardcover coffee-table books make a great surface to elevate your pedal so you can reach it more easily. Just make sure there's enough room on the book(s) for your heel to rest too, so you can relax from time to time.

on the floor so you can fully press down the pedal if necessary and with no strain. Now that you're adjusted properly, you will be able to spend hours and hours quilting without the aches and pains that troubled me in my early months of quilting.

Sit at the proper height so your elbows make a 90° angle when your palms are flat on the surface of your extension table.

Prepping Your Project

Preparing your quilt or other project properly is the foundation for successful quilting. If seam allowances aren't properly pressed, you'll struggle to quilt over them later. If your quilt isn't adequately basted, then you'll deal with a whole host of problems while quilting it. These tasks are mundane, but necessary. If you're going to do something mundane, it's best to do it right the first time so it doesn't come back to haunt you later . . . right? Right.

PRESSING

Before basting your project, make sure the quilt top and backing fabric are properly pressed. I like to use steam on a cotton setting and do more of a steam and press than a gliding motion. This way I don't stress the seams or stretch bias edges out of shape. I also recommend pressing seam allowances open if at all possible. Seam intersections are a common place for your darning foot to become stuck and for things to go awry. It has happened to me on more than one occasion—it's frustrating and doesn't look very pretty. So press those seam allowances open while piecing and spare yourself the headache.

BASTING

I prepare my projects using one of three different basting methods—pin basting, spray basting, and fusible-fleece basting. Which method I choose depends on several factors. Take time to read about each method and select the best type of basting for the quilt or other project you're making. Good basting will seriously improve the look of your free-motion quilting, while also making the quilting much easier to do, so it's worth taking the time to learn how to do it right. The first choice you need to make is which type of batting you will use.

Batting Choices

You'll find a wide array of batting these days, from polyester to bamboo, wool, and cotton—as well as blends. There's even organic batting. And that's not to mention the various lofts (thicknesses) available. The choices can be quite overwhelming. I use the same batting in all my projects because it works well, washes well, wears well, it doesn't shrink, and it's lightweight but warm. In my mind, it is a perfect product that needs no improvement. My preferred batting is Fairfield 80% cotton and 20% polyester blend. Many quilters are fans of the crinkled look. I'm not one of those quilters. I don't like my batting to shrink, because my quilting designs are less visible underneath the puckered fabric. Therefore, I use this batting to achieve the lightness and feel of cotton, without the shrinkage. The polyester gives it added strength, too, making it a good choice for even fine, tightly stitched free-motion quilting.

When choosing batting, there are a few things to consider. What is the shrinkage and how will it need to be laundered? What is the strength, and what quilting distance is recommended? Some battings allow for very large-scale quilting, while others require quilting stitches to be no more than an inch or two apart. Another factor to consider is loft. I like a low loft, as it allows the best view of the free-motion quilting. High-loft battings will hide some of the stitching. All these factors boil down to preference and project suitability. It's important to choose a well-rounded batting and stick with it. Or, make careful selections on a project-by-project basis, making sure to do your research so there are no surprises later.

Pin Basting

Pin basting is a fail-safe method—it's tried and true. When I first started free-motion quilting, it was the only method I ever used. If you're going to use only one basting method, this is the one to learn. For pin basting you'll need lots of curved safety pins, masking tape or painter's tape, and a clean, flat surface to tape the back of your quilt to. I have tile floors in my house, so I just clear out my dining-room table and rug when I need to pin baste a large quilt and do it on the tile. If you only have carpeted surfaces, you may want to invest in a few folding banquet tables to use as a basting surface.

1. Start by laying your backing wrong side up on a clean, flat surface and smoothing out all the wrinkles. Using masking tape, tape the backing to the floor or table, starting in the middle on one side. Move to the opposite side of the backing, very gently pull the backing taut, and tape it down. Move to the middle of an untaped side, very gently pull the backing taut, and tape it down. Move to the last side, gently pull the backing taut, and tape it down. Work your way around the quilt in the same manner, taping the backing to the floor or table about every 6" to 8", always moving opposite of where you just taped, and gently pulling the backing taut before taping it down.

2. Once the backing is evenly taped to the floor or table on all sides, you're ready to lay out the batting. Take your batting out of the package and tumble it in the dryer with a few damp washcloths and dryer sheets on the fluff or air setting for about 15 minutes. This really helps reduce the wrinkles and static in the batting. Or, you can take it out of the package the day before and fluff it out to let the creases relax.

3. Center the batting on top of the backing. Starting in the center, gently smooth out the wrinkles, generally "sticking" the batting to the backing fabric by patting it in place. Take your time and get out all creases, pleats, and wrinkles. Don't pull or stretch the batting. If you need to readjust the batting, gently loft it up and down to get it straight on the backing.

4. Center your pressed quilt top over the batting. Again, smooth out all the pleats and wrinkles, taking your time to smooth over each area several times—really sticking the quilt top to the batting. The backing and batting should be 2" larger than your quilt top on all sides. If it's any smaller and the layers shift while quilting, the backing might not cover part of your quilt. If you have more than 2" of backing and batting, it's just unnecessary bulk for you to move around while quilting. (You can trim the batting and backing after basting the layers.)

Pin basting

5. Starting in the center, place pins every 4", or even closer. Place the pins in rows, working from the center out to one side and then from the center out to the other side. Pin a row above the middle and then pin one below the middle. Basting this way will help keep the layers even and straight. I use my hand as a guide for pinning; edge to edge across my knuckles is about 4", making it the perfect, always-accessible spacer.

6. Once the entire quilt is covered edge to edge with pins, remove the tape and trim the batting and backing as needed, making sure to leave 2" on all sides of your quilt top.

The main benefit of pin basting is that you don't use chemicals in this process. If you're sensitive to chemicals, you could theoretically buy organic fabric, batting, and thread, and pin baste; then you wouldn't have any yucky stuff to deal with. The disadvantage of pin basting is the huge amount of time it takes, as well as the necessity for a hard, flat surface larger than your quilt.

Spray Basting

Spray basting is a time-saver in a can—literally! While it may take me two to three hours to pin baste a queen-size quilt, I can spray baste the same quilt in about 45 minutes. Interested in learning more? I bet you are!

A few different companies make spray baste, but I like SprayNBond basting adhesive by Therm O Web because it's odorless and the overspray is very minimal. If you do have any overspray, it's easy to clean with soap and water, which is a bonus. I especially like to use this method for small projects.

I spray baste by hanging my quilt on a wall. First, I hang up some newspaper roughly around the area where my backing will be, which makes cleanup a breeze. I then tack the quilt backing to the wall, with the right side facing the wall, using thumbtacks every few inches across the top edge of the fabric and making sure the backing is smooth and flat. Then, after laying more newspaper on the floor beneath the backing, I spray baste following the manufacturer's instructions.

As with pin basting, I tumble the batting in the dryer for about 15 minutes. Once the backing is lightly coated, I remove the batting from the dryer and, starting along the top edge, I carefully pat the batting in place. The great thing about SprayNBond is that it is truly repositionable. I have repositioned batting over and over in certain areas and it stuck right back down. Take your time to carefully position and stick the batting to the backing, making sure the batting is smooth. Once the batting is in place, spray the batting and adhere the quilt top to the batting in the same way. And that's it! It's a very fast and easy process—and quite addictive if I do say so myself.

Spray basting

But there are disadvantages to spray basting, too. You have those chemicals, so if the project is for a baby or a bed pillow, you may want to choose a different basting method or wash the project after it's finished to remove the basting spray. Also, the adhesive is temporary. I coat my projects well with basting spray and it usually lasts a few days before it starts losing its tackiness. This is why I don't typically spray baste big quilts: I may not finish quilting them before the spray loses its effectiveness. But this is my go-to method for smaller projects or quilts that I know I will quilt in a few days or less.

Fusible-Fleece Basting

The last method of basting involves fusible fleece. For certain projects in this book, I highly recommend using fusible fleece for best results. I like to use HeatNBond high-loft iron-on fusible fleece by Therm O Web instead of interfacing when I construct purses and bags. I like making quilted bags, and this product acts like batting for a quilted look, but has the rigidity and sturdiness of interfacing. It's heavy and strong—more like felt than batting—and one side is fusible. I always fuse it to the outer layer of my project and then use basting spray to adhere the backing. The disadvantage of this type of basting is its limited use—unless you're looking for something stiffer and more sturdy. This isn't the method I use for a typical quilt.

Fusible-fleece basting

Thread and Tension

Let me tell you a little story about thread that I think perfectly sums up my thoughts on the subject. Once upon a time, I was a stubborn and very thrifty brand-new free-motion quilter, who scoffed at the idea of paying high prices for premium thread. I had no trouble using my cones of serger thread for quilting. Although they created a lot more lint for me to deal with, they were a fraction of the price of premium thread, and so I laughed all the way to the bank—or so I thought.

Fast-forward a few years, and I was still quilting with my inexpensive serger thread when I decided it was time to finally tackle the challenge of making a queen-size quilt for my bed. I only had my small domestic sewing machine with an average throat size (the amount of space to the right of the needle). Quilting that quilt was a major challenge. I literally sweated over that quilt for weeks. Once it was finished, I couldn't have been prouder—cheap thread and all. It looked beautiful. I couldn't wait to get it on our bed. By the time it had been on the bed for about a year, the thread literally disintegrated. It was the biggest tragedy I've seen in my quilting career so far. My beautiful quilt, to which I'd devoted hours and hours of free-motion quilting, was falling apart in front of my eyes.

What's more, the difference in cost of quality thread versus what I used would have been about $10. That's all. I could have saved myself a major heartache and had an heirloom to enjoy forever instead of a fleeting and painful lesson. Don't be stubborn like me. Learn where to spend your money and where to save it when quilting. Thread is not the thing to scrimp on when it comes to free-motion quilting.

QUALITY THREAD

So what constitutes a quality thread for free-motion quilting? Good-quality machine-quilting thread is designed to be used at high speeds and endure the stresses of free-motion quilting. The stresses include lots of stretching as you move the quilt around, and lines of stitching being stitched over multiple times, which can shred and fray poor-quality thread. There are lots of thread options, and you don't have to limit yourself to those specified for machine quilting. High-quality embroidery thread is also designed to

be used at high speed and stitched over multiple times, and I have had much success using it for free-motion quilting.

When starting with free-motion quilting, I recommend choosing one brand of thread that offers a wide range of colors and is known to be high quality. Once you've chosen it, stick with it. That way you can figure out how to set up your machine's tension for that thread and keep it consistent every time. This will save you lots of trouble and make quilting less stressful. Two brands I have used extensively and really like are Isacord and Aurifil. Isacord is a 40-weight polyester embroidery thread. It comes in an excellent range of colors and works great for free-motion quilting. It is very cost-effective and a great thread to use as a beginner. Aurifil is my top choice in thread—I love the Mako 40-weight cotton thread. It has an extensive range of colors and is the highest quality.

TENSION

Tension is a very important part of preparing for free-motion quilting. The goal is to set the tension on your machine to give you the best quilting stitches with the least possible amount of frustration. Bad tension results in a number of problems, such as bird's nests on the front or back of your quilt, thread breakage, and loose, sloppy-looking stitches that you'll just end up ripping out anyway—in short, headaches. You get the idea. It's so much better to just get it right the first time. It's very easy to see if your tension is good or bad by simply stitching on a practice sandwich with the feed dogs dropped. Stitch a straight line and a wiggly line and then stop to examine the stitching closely. If the tension is correct, all the stitches will sink into the middle (both the top and the back will be indented evenly), you won't see any bobbin thread coming through the top in the form of tiny loops, and you won't see any thread lying on the surface of the fabric instead of sunken into the batting layer like it should be. If the tension isn't perfectly balanced, you'll need to make adjustments. I know perfection can be frustrating, but this is the one time I am going to tell you it isn't optional. Get it right—you'll thank me later.

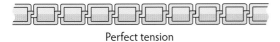

Perfect tension

Tension too loose. If the bobbin thread is lying flat on the back of the quilt or is slightly sunken in but not to the middle of the batting, this means your tension is too loose. Make small adjustments toward a higher number. Continue stitching samples and checking the tension until all the stitches come together in the middle of the batting.

Tension too tight. If you can see your bobbin thread poking through to the top layer, then your tension is too tight and you need to use a lower number. This is the more common of the two problems, as typically a sewing machine's tension needs to be loosened a bit for free-motion quilting.

To make testing your tension even easier, use a different-colored thread of the exact same brand and weight in the bobbin than in the machine needle. It makes it very easy to see if the bobbin thread is coming up through the top. Once you have your tension set perfectly, consider using a permanent marker to mark your sewing machine at that setting; that way you will always know just where to set it when it is time to quilt. Choosing one brand and blend of thread and sticking with it will allow you to never fuss with the tension—once thread weight or brand is changed, you'll need to perform another tension test. I recommend always using the same thread in the bobbin that you use in the needle. If you use another color, or worse yet a different type or weight of thread, you will surely experience frustrations. Once your tension is all set to quilt, you can relax and know that one of the things that plagues new quilters the most won't be bothering you any more!

Make a Tension Sample

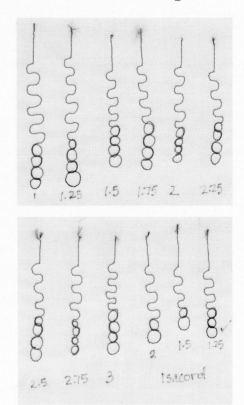

Using Isacord thread, with navy on the top and red in the bobbin, I could easily identify the top and bottom threads in my tension sample. For this thread, a very low tension setting of 1.25 was best for my machine.

When the tension is set correctly, the red bottom thread does not show through very much to the top and isn't pulled up in the curved areas. When the tension setting is too high, the red bobbin thread pulls at the corners and the navy thread sits on the surface instead of sinking into the fabric.

Sketching

What if I knew a secret that would make you a better quilter much faster, would you want to know it? If success was guaranteed, would it be a technique you would definitely use? I thought so.

The best way to see quick improvement in your free-motion quilting is to spend any free moment you can sketching the designs you are trying to learn. I have boxes of scrap papers, sketchbooks, notebooks, and anything else I could get my mitts on filled to the brim with sketched free-motion designs. The more the better! When you sketch a design in continuous-line form (without letting the tip of your pen leave the paper), you're doing two very crucial things that will benefit you greatly when it comes to stitching the same design. The first thing you're doing is building muscle memory for that design—the more your hands and brain work together to create the design with the challenge of keeping it a continuous line, the more natural it becomes, and eventually you don't even have to think about it. You can just stipple or pebble or swirl with ultimate ease. It takes a long time to get to that place, so if you rely only on quilting as practice, it will take tons of fabric, batting, and thread to gain that experience. That's why sketching is so great!

The second thing you'll learn by sketching is how to spatially organize the design—meaning how to fill the space properly, how to keep the size and scale consistent, how to change scale and keep that consistent, how to combine designs, and so on. Again, these lessons are invaluable and would be much harder and longer to learn if practiced only on the sewing machine.

Consider a fine artist; let's use an oil painter as an example. When first learning the craft of painting, the artist was surely taught to take time to sketch

In these selections from my sketchbooks, you can see how I combine designs on paper before quilting them on fabric.

and plan out his or her paintings instead of just plopping paint on a canvas and going for it. The same thing applies to free-motion quilting. Careful planning and consideration of what designs to use where will give your quilt a customized, professional look, no matter what your skill level. And by drawing quilt blocks or designs and then sketching different variations of the quilting designs on top of them, you can get the most out of the designs you know and the skills you have.

I recommend sketching with a fine-point permanent marker. That way you can't erase your lines. Just as I don't want you to spend time unpicking stitches while learning free-motion quilting, I don't find it productive to erase your sketching. The goal isn't perfection; it's muscle memory and spatial planning. If you remember that and just relax and have fun with your quilting (and sketching!), you won't be afraid to get creative.

Here are a few examples from my sketchbook to give you an idea of what combining designs and playing with the scale can look like.

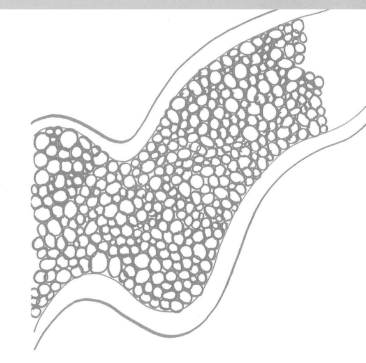

Five Prep Steps for Free-Motion Quilting

With free-motion quilting, repetition is key, especially when it comes to remembering to put the correct presser foot on your machine or drop the feed dogs! Though these simple steps may seem obvious, you'd be surprised how many times I've been so excited to start quilting something that I forgot to adjust my tension or drop my feed dogs, and I ended up with some bad-looking stitches. Sometimes I figure out my mistake right away, but one time in particular I was quilting my very first paper-pieced block (circle of geese!). In my eagerness to get started, I forgot to drop the feed dogs. I was doing really tiny pebbles and didn't notice my mistake until I was half finished and the back looked less than beautiful. Luckily, I was making it into a pillow so the back wouldn't be seen, but if it had been a quilt I probably would have had to rip out thousands of tiny stitches—no fun!

So let's make repetition our motto and remember to execute these five steps every single time:

1. **Clean and oil your machine.** Check the needle and replace it if necessary. I know it's no fun, but your sewing machine is your partner in this new free-motion quilting venture, and to function at her best she needs regular maintenance. When free-motion quilting, I always clean and oil my machine during every other bobbin change. Though it's a pain when I just want to get that project done, I have been free-motion quilting heavily as well as piecing for the past five years, and with my regular every-other-bobbin maintenance I have avoided needing to have my machine serviced. Five years later, my machine runs just like she did when I got her! When I think about that, all the cleaning and oiling was definitely worth it.

   Note: Not all machines require oiling or can be disassembled for cleaning. Consult your user's manual if you aren't certain, and regardless of the type of machine, always keep your bobbin area lint-free using a small nylon brush.

Make sure to remove the cover plate and clean out all the lint in your machine.

2. **Fill a few bobbins** (depending on the size of your project) and thread your machine with good-quality machine-quilting thread. Use matching thread in the bobbin.

3. **Lower the feed dogs.** Feed dogs are the little serrated bars that move up and down beneath your needle plate. They help guide the fabric forward as you sew. When free-motion quilting, you want to lower the feed dogs so *you* control all the fabric movement. Most machines have a button or switch that lowers the feed dogs; consult your manual if you are unsure how to do it. If you plan on using a Supreme Slider (see page 10), now is the time to put that on too.

   If your machine doesn't allow you to lower the feed dogs, fear not! You can still free-motion quilt. When the feed dogs can't be lowered, some machines come with a plate that covers the feed dogs. Look through your manual and accessories to see if you have a plate cover. If you don't have one, look at the available accessories to see if you can purchase one. You can also use a piece of cardstock or a business card to cover the feed dogs. Punch a hole in the center of the card so you have a place for your needle to go through. Then line up the card and needle so the needle doesn't hit the sides of the hole, and tape the card over the feed dogs. In this situation, I strongly suggest using a

Supreme Slider, because you can cover the card with the Supreme Slider and have a nice, slick working surface. Eventually the card will wear out from rubbing against the feed dogs. Check the card every time you change the bobbin and replace it as needed.

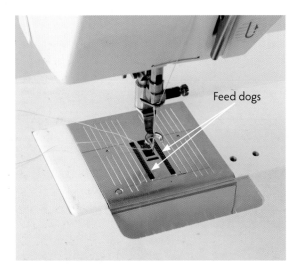

Lower the feed dogs so you are in control of moving the fabric.

4. **Swap out your regular presser foot** for an open- or closed-toe darning foot, and you are almost ready to go! Don't forget to put on your quilting gloves if you use them.

Where to Start

For quilting designs such as stippling, pebbling, and swirls, I recommend starting in the center of the practice square or project. When quilting an edge-to-edge design such as wood grain, loop de loops, handwriting, square meander, nesting boxes, or paisley, I recommend starting on an outer edge.

5. **Put the section of your project** where you want to start quilting under the needle. Lower the presser foot and, using the hand wheel or the needle up/down button if you have one, sink the needle down into the fabric and then let it come all the way back up. Gently tug the thread tail until the bobbin thread loops up through the surface of your quilt. Pull on that

loop until the bobbin tail is all the way on the surface. Now you are ready to begin.

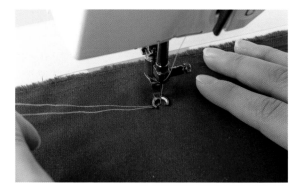

Pull the bobbin thread up to the top to avoid any tangles or bird's nests on the quilt back.

Practice Squares

These squares are for practice, so you won't want to use expensive fabrics, but some fabrics are more suitable than others.

- Avoid busy prints. Solids or low-contrast prints are less distracting and will let you see your quilting.
- Use 100% cotton fabric. You want to simulate quilting a real quilt, so choose muslin or cotton broadcloth.
- Look in the clearance section. The fabrics don't have to be pretty—they're for practice.
- Use leftover batting scraps. You can piece together leftovers from other projects by butting their edges and zigzag stitching them together to use in your practice squares.

Making the squares: Cut two 12" squares of fabric and one of batting. Layer them with the batting in the middle. You don't need to bother basting them; just smooth the layers together and they'll stay put.

Mark a line 1" from all outer edges to define a 10" square; sew on the marked line. The stitching will secure your practice square, give you a space in which to quilt, provide an edge to work from, and give you room to maintain proper hand position for maximum control.

Tips, Tricks, and Reminders

Although there are no miracle tricks to make you an overnight quilting sensation, there are a few things I have learned along the way that I wish I had known from the start. I hope these are as helpful to you as I think they might have been to me when I was beginning my quilting journey.

Relax. Your quilting will look better. Seriously. A stressed-out quilter who is nervous and has tight shoulders and a clenched jaw will quilt jagged, sharp lines. A relaxed quilter with soft shoulders and a relaxed jaw will be free to curve and move. Honestly, any tension you are holding will show in your quilting, so put on some good music or a book on tape, make sure you are comfortable, and take lots of breaks. If you feel stressed and anxious, it's not a good time to quilt.

Draw a lot. I know we covered it, but it's that important. So do it.

Don't be afraid to fail. Don't worry about ruining your beautiful work with bad quilting. You have to start somewhere, and there is absolutely NO WAY to avoid being a beginner when you are beginning something. I know it isn't fun to be imperfect, but you need to learn in order to grow and get better. And you won't learn unless you practice on actual quilts and quilted items.

Celebrate the victories! This is a journey with highs and lows. You will surely stress out about the lows, which is only human nature. Don't forget about the victories, though. Praise yourself for improvement and show off your work. Be proud of it. If you balance the tough moments of learning this skill with the victorious ones, you'll give yourself the motivation to keep working at it.

Take your shoes off. What? Wait, did she just tell me to take my shoes off? Well, yes I did! And I have good reason—I promise. One of the things your body and brain need to learn is how to control the speed of your sewing machine and time it to the movements of your hands. That sounds harder than

it is. The reason you want to quilt in bare or stocking feet is because you can feel the subtle nuances of the speed control in your foot pedal. While wearing shoes you'd be lucky to get three speeds—slow, medium, and holy-cow-slow-down turbo! A common misconception is that to quilt well you need to sew fast. This couldn't be further from the truth.

To free-motion quilt well, you need to be able to slow down and speed up. If you move your hands faster than your needle is moving, you'll get long stitches. If you're moving too fast and in a circular motion, you can cause tension issues. If you move your hands too slowly and your needle is going fast, then you'll stitch teeny-tiny stitches. You want a good balance, somewhere in the middle. This isn't something to stress about, and please don't go out and buy a stitch regulator under the delusion that perfect stitch length will surely make you a better quilter. It will just mean you have perfect stitch length. If you aren't good at quilting the designs, they won't look good. It's best to practice moving your hands in harmony with the speed of the machine. Quilting without shoes will help.

Start and stop. When starting or stopping in the center of a project, always sew five or six stitches in place to secure the threads. Remove your quilt from the machine and clip the thread tails close to the quilt top.

Set a realistic goal. Strive for improvement, not perfection. Remember that when you're feeling judgmental of your work. Resist the urge to rip out stitches. Some quilters spend half their quilting time ripping out whatever they've stitched because their impossibly high standards deem it imperfect. Talk about an exercise in frustration. It's called "free motion" for a reason. You, an imperfect human, will be doing all the controlling of movements, so guess what—there will be imperfections. Even the world's best quilter could point out her own mistakes. You may never notice them, but she knows just where they are. So accept that you'll be imperfect and that you'll improve with practice. And keep that wonky stitching intact as a reminder of just where you were at that point in your journey. Unless the quilt is bound for a juried quilt show, there is no reason to rip out your quilting as long as it's functional.

Loop de Loops and Handwriting

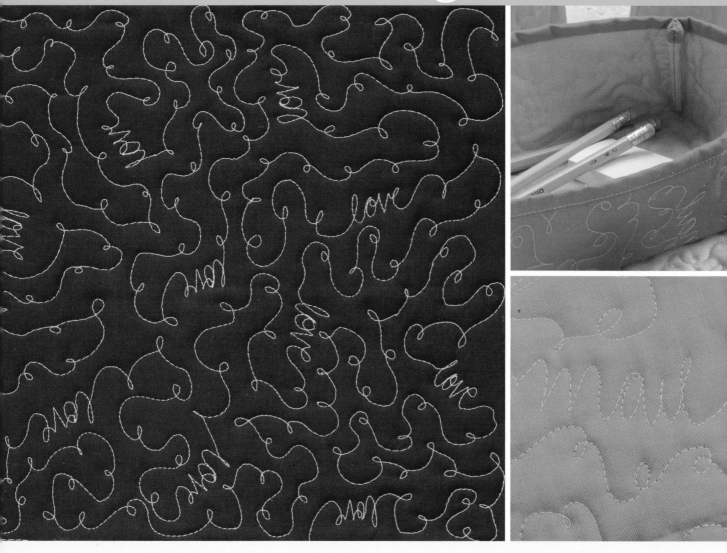

When choosing what type of quilting pattern to start with, I thought back to my very first attempts at free-motion quilting, and what worked well for me and what I struggled with. I also thought about friends and students who have told me about their first moments of free-motion quilting. It seems the general feeling we all shared was trepidation. What do I do first? Where do I start? You are learning many brand-new things during the first moments of free-motion quilting, and it's a whole lot for even the best multitasker to manage. When I first sat down and tried free-motion quilting, I started with classic stippling, because I thought I was supposed to start there. It turned out that wasn't a good starting point for me because the movements were so foreign. That, combined with all the other things my brain was trying to keep track of, became overwhelming and ultimately led to frustration.

I took a deep breath and thought, I know how to write my name, why not try to quilt that? I started with just a letter *e*, then a lowercase *l* in classic grade-school cursive, where all the letters are connected. It was going much more smoothly for me than my stippling, and it looked much better, too. So I went for my whole first and last name, and shocked myself when it looked almost as good as if I had written it with a marker! Drawing on that experience, I'm asking you all to start at the same place. We all have the muscle memory for basic cursive writing. You don't need to think very hard about what to do next, as everyone knows how to form letters. I've found that using the basic loop de loop (which is just like stitching a cursive letter *e*) allows you the freedom to add text—whatever quilted word you like—and works extremely well as a quilting design. This pattern works really well to enhance any theme in quilting or to help express a message. The options for personalization are endless. Let's get started!

INSTRUCTIONS

1. Set up your machine following "Five Prep Steps for Free-Motion Quilting" on page 21, and prepare a practice square.

2. Making sure your hands are in the proper position for maximum fabric control, slowly sew five or six stitches in place before slowly stitching a lowercase cursive *e*. Continue to quilt another *e*, followed by a third all in a row.

3. Continue with your row of letters and try adding a lowercase *l*. Quilt several more in a row.

4. When you come to the end of your first row, quilt a line under the quilted row of letters that will bring you back to the left edge. Begin a new row, this time starting with the letter *m* and then a *w*.

5. Continue trying new letters, such as an *o*. Attempt to quilt your name or another easy word. One of my favorite words to quilt is *love*.

6. Branch out from the rows and start trying to fill your space with loop de loops, leaving ½" to 1" between loops.

7. After filling some space with plain loop de loops, add a word such as your name or the word *love*. Continue practicing in this way. Every letter you master is a shape or movement you can refer to later as you are learning more designs.

Remember to Stop Often

When starting out, one of the most common mistakes new quilters make is forgetting to stop and reposition their hands. This means your hands aren't in the best place for fabric control, and you're in danger of losing control of the fabric as well as getting your hand dangerously close to the needle. Every few inches, slow to a stop, reposition your hands, and then continue quilting. Getting in this habit early on will make the whole learning process much easier.

Organize It Bowl Set

Pieced and quilted by Molly Hanson

Organization isn't a strong suit for me, especially when it comes time to gathering essentials to leave the house. Where are those darned keys? Have you seen my wallet? How about the phone? You get the picture. I designed these cute little organizing bowls as the perfect solution to that problem. I had fun with the quilting, working in some words with my loops. The words may help me keep things in their proper place, and they look cute too! This set is useful for organizing your bathroom, your sewing room—or wherever there's clutter!

FINISHED SIZES
Small bowls: 5" x 5"
Large bowl: 5" x 10"
Tray: 11" x 11"

MATERIALS
Yardage is based on 42"-wide fabric. Fat quarters measure 18" x 21".

8 fat quarters of assorted solids (2 fat quarters for each bowl and for the tray)

Batting: 1 square, 16" x 16"
2 squares, 11" x 11"
1 rectangle, 11" x 15½"

INSTRUCTIONS

Press the fat quarters and arrange them in pairs according to your choice of colors. One piece will be the outside of your bowl or tray; the other will be the inside. Keep this in mind as you work through the project.

Small Bowls

1. From two fat-quarter sets, cut a total of four squares, 11" x 11".

2. Layer each set of fat-quarter squares with an 11" square of batting; baste.

3. Quilt as shown in the quilting map.

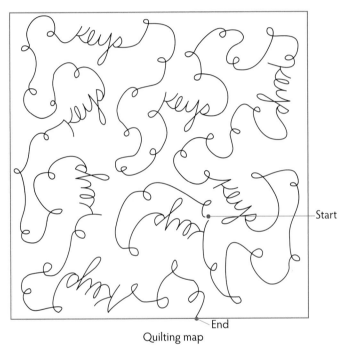

Quilting map

4. Trim each quilted square to measure 9½" x 9½".

5. Mark a 2" square in each corner of a quilted piece as shown and cut out the squares on the marked lines.

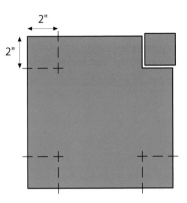

6. Refer to "Binding" on page 94. From the leftover fat-quarter fabric, cut four 2" x 5½" strips and bind the edges as shown. *Do not bind the 2"-long edges in the corners.*

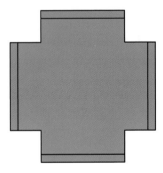

7. In one corner, match the two raw edges as shown, making sure to place the fabric you want on the inside of the bowl right sides together. Sew a scant ¼" seam. Turn the bowl inside out, press along the seamline, and sew ¼" from the

folded edge to enclose the first seam. The raw edges are now buried inside the seam. Repeat for the other three corners.

Align raw edges.

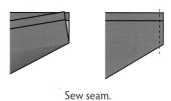

Sew seam.

Raw edge

Turn inside out and sew.

8. Repeat steps 5–7 to make a second small bowl.

Large Bowl

For detailed instructions and illustrations, refer to "Small Bowls" on page 27.

1. From one fat-quarter set, cut two 11" x 15½" rectangles. Layer the fabric rectangles with an 11" x 15½" rectangle of batting; baste.

2. Quilt as shown in the quilting map. Trim the quilted rectangle to measure 9½" x 14".

3. Mark a 2" square in each corner and cut out the squares. Bind the edges and finish the corners.

Tray

For detailed instructions and illustrations, refer to "Small Bowls" on page 27.

1. From the remaining fat-quarter set, cut two 16" squares. Layer the fabric squares with a 16" square of batting; baste.

2. Quilt as shown in the quilting map. Trim the quilted square to measure 14" x 14".

3. Mark a 1" square in each corner and cut out the squares. Bind the edges and finish the corners.

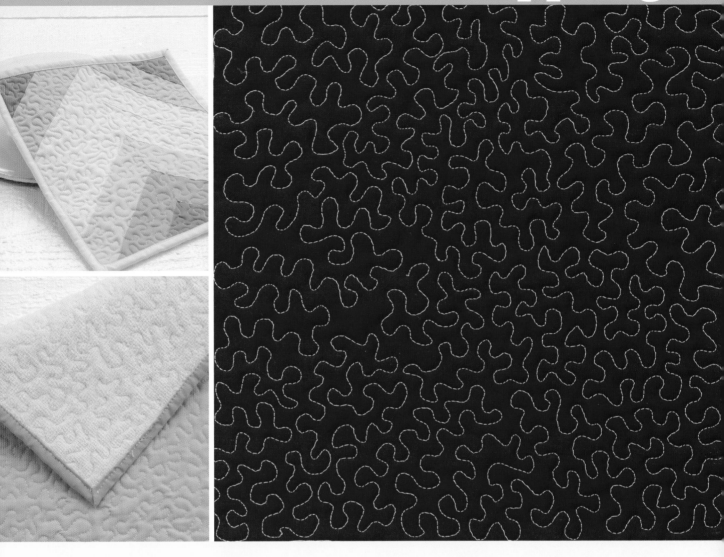

The basic stipple, or meander stitch as it is often referred to, is far and away the single most commonly used design in free-motion quilting. Its versatility, light texture, and ability to blend and not compete with the piecing make it a favorite among quilters of every era and generation. There are many quilters who never learn, or use, another design beyond stippling. If you were going to master only one quilting design, this is definitely the one. (Not that I in any way advocate stopping your free-motion quilting education at only *one* design!)

This design is based on a few simple rules. Essentially, you are stitching curvy U-shaped lines and never crossing over them. This means you'll fill your space with horseshoe-like curves, while moving your quilt in such a way that you don't quilt into a corner (or area) that you can't quilt out of without crossing over a previous line of stitching.

This is a design that can take minutes to learn and a lifetime to master. It takes lots of practice to maintain a consistent scale and keep your lines curved.

Stippling is a random type of design with no general path of movement required, so you may often find your brain becoming stuck. With so many options and directions to move in, it is sometimes overwhelming. To combat this, I focus on quilting in waves of movements. I hesitate to say "rows" because I generally start with a cluster of stippling in the center of my project, and then work outward toward an edge in back-and-forth sweeping waves. I make sure to fill all the space as I go so that I don't leave any holes I have to fill in later.

Try drawing stippling patterns in this fashion before attempting to quilt them. Several pages filled with drawn stippling will really aid you in the learning process.

INSTRUCTIONS

1. Set up your machine following "Five Prep Steps for Free-Motion Quilting" on page 21, and prepare a practice square.

2. Making sure your hands are in the proper place for maximum fabric control, slowly sew five or six stitches in place before quilting a *U* shape. Immediately move into another *U* and try quilting a row of wiggly *U* shapes as shown.

3. When you're nearing the edge of your practice square, quilt in a downward direction and fill another area with more random *U* shapes. Think of jigsaw-puzzle pieces with their U-shaped edges going every which way. Make some of the *U* shapes pointed upward and some downward, and then some going left to right. Varying the direction will improve the look of the design.

4. Continue filling your square with stippling. When you're done, take the time to fill several more pages of your sketchbook with stippling, to really help your brain learn the movements.

5. Try another practice square and see how much easier it is once your brain has a better understanding of how to create this design. Keep practicing, drawing, and quilting this design.

Quilting Out of a Corner

Find yourself quilted into a corner? Don't worry! You have a couple options: You can break the rules and cross over a line of stitching. Or you can break the thread and move to a new area of your project, start again, and keep going. Don't let little hiccups frustrate you. Just keep quilting!

Chevron Tea Towel and Pot Holder

Pieced and quilted by Molly Hanson

FINISHED SIZES

Tea towel: 14" x 25"
Pot holder: 10" x 11"

MATERIALS

Yardage is based on 42"-wide fabric and is sufficient for 1 tea towel and 1 pot holder. A fat quarter measures 18" x 21".

1 velveteen-type bath towel, 25" x 50" or larger, for towel backing*

1 fat quarter of beige solid for tea towel

7 strips, 2" x 42", of assorted green solids for patchwork

4 strips, 2½" x 42", of green solid for binding

You'll have enough bath towel left over to make another tea towel, if desired.

Did you know that towels make an excellent substitute for batting and backing and can be quilted? A velveteen-type towel—thin weight with a short velvet pile on one side and a longer loop pile on the other—is the way to go! For this project, you'll turn one bath towel into a tea towel (or two) with patchwork accents. The project dimensions are based on the width of my towel. If you have a larger or smaller towel, simply adjust the dimensions. The pot holder uses the leftover strip set from the tea towel. The set goes together super quick and makes a functional, pretty gift. I call that a win-win!

MAKING THE CHEVRON

1. Cut each assorted green 2"-wide strip in half to make 14 strips, 2" x 21". Lay out seven green strips in the order you desire. Staggering the ends by 2", sew the strips together along their long edges to make a strip set. Press the seam allowances toward the top strip. Lay out a second set of seven green strips, making sure they are a mirror image of the first strip set. Join the strips in the same way as before. Press the seam allowances toward the bottom strip.

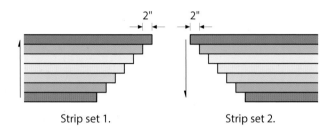

Strip set 1.   Strip set 2.

2. Layer the strip sets right sides together. Using a rotary cutter and a ruler with 45° markings, align the 45° line with a seamline on the strip set as shown. Trim off the irregular end of the strip set. *Do not* separate the strip sets.

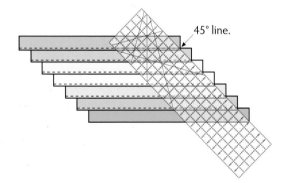

45° line.

3. With your strip sets still right sides together, rotate the strips 180°. Measure 2" from the freshly cut end of the strip set and cut a 2"-wide segment. Be sure to handle the bias edges gently to avoid stretching.

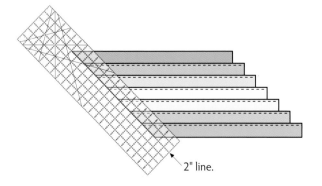

2" line.

4. Butt the seam intersections up against each other and pin at each seamline. Sew the strips together. Press the seam allowances open. Trim the strip to measure 3½" x 14".

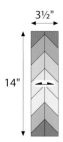

3½"

14"

TEA TOWEL

1. Trim the beige fat quarter to measure 14" x 22". Sew the chevron strip you just completed to one short end to complete the towel top. Press the seam allowances open.

2. From the bath towel, cut a piece that is 1" to 2" larger on all sides than the towel top. Spray baste the towel top to the loop side of the towel.

3. Quilt as shown in the quilting map.

End

Start
Start

End

Quilting map

4. Trim the edges of the towel even with the edges of the top. Referring to "Binding" on page 94, bind the edges using two of the green 2½"-wide strips.

POT HOLDER

Use the leftovers of the strip sets from "Making the Chevron" on page 32.

Additional Materials

12" x 12" square of fabric for backing

12" x 12" piece of Insul-brite heat-proof batting

12" x 12" piece of regular batting

Instructions

1. Refer to "Making the Chevron," steps 2 and 3 on page 32. Layer the strip sets, right sides together, and trim the end. *Do not* separate the strip sets. Measure 5" from the freshly cut end and cut a 5"-wide segment. *Do not* separate the segments.

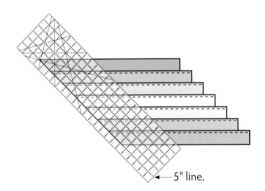

5" line.

2. Pin and sew the segments together along one long edge, making sure to match the seam intersections. Press the seam allowances open.

3. Trim the piece to measure 11" x 11", taking time to line up your cuts so you get as much of the pretty chevron as possible.

4. Following the manufacturer's instructions, spray baste the Insul-brite to the wrong side of the chevron piece. Spray baste the piece of regular batting to the Insul-brite. Then, spray baste the wrong side of the backing to the batting.

5. Quilt as shown in the quilting map.

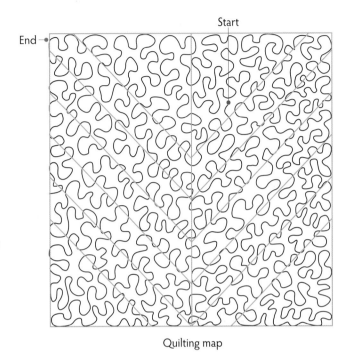

Quilting map

6. Trim the pot holder to measure 10" x 11".

7. Referring to "Binding" on page 94 and using the two remaining green 2½"-wide strips, bind the edges. For this project, start sewing the binding in the upper-right or upper-left corner, whichever you prefer. Stop stitching ½" from where you started. Trim the binding end, leaving about 3". Making sure the raw edges are tucked inside and starting at the edge of the pot holder, sew the binding tail closed. Fold the binding to form a loop and tuck the end into the ½" opening. Sew the opening closed.

Pebbles and Chain of Pearls

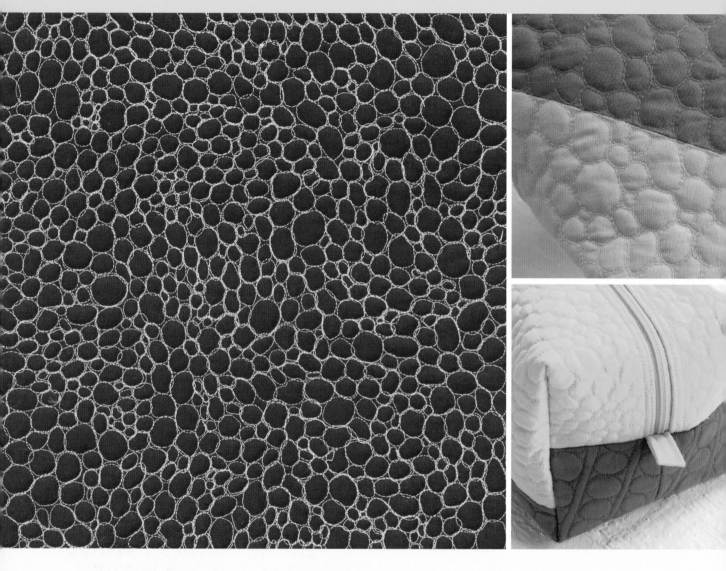

Whether you call them pebbles, bubbles, or pearls, chances are you are talking about a quilting design consisting of a space filled with as many touching circles as possible. It's one of my favorite quilting designs and definitely the design that has earned me the most compliments. People just seem to love the look and texture of pebbles. I can't blame them—I do too!

Pebbles, like stippling, can fit in just about anywhere. Even a single row of pebbles, called a "chain of pearls," can be beautiful when squeezed into a tiny border or the spine of a feather. The quilting designs I use most frequently are an allover pebble fill and a chain of pearls, and I bet many quilters would say the same thing. These designs take time to master, but their usefulness is worth the effort.

That said, pebbles are a labor of love and you'd do well to remember that before committing to quilting pebbles over a very large surface. Pebbles take longer to quilt than any other design and use more thread too. You often have to stitch around each pebble once or even twice to move to where you need to go to make your next pebble. I like to combine pebbles with other fill designs, as it always creates an interesting contrast and limits the areas I pebble.

INSTRUCTIONS

1. Set up your machine following "Five Prep Steps for Free-Motion Quilting" on page 21, and prepare a practice square.

2. Making sure your hands are in the proper position for maximum fabric control, sew five or six stitches in place before slowly stitching a ½"-diameter circle. Stop where you started. Slowly and carefully sew on top of your previous stitching in a clockwise direction until you reach the right side of your circle. Then branch out to make another circle right next to the first one.

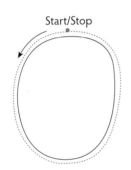

Start/Stop

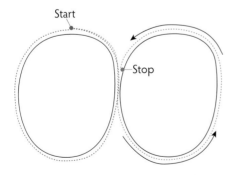

Start

Stop

3. Stop where you started your second circle. You should be on the far left side of the second circle. Quilt over the top of the second circle to get to the opposite side of the circle, and quilt another circle butting up against the second one. Continue in the same manner, making a chain of pearls or a row of circles.

4. Once you have completed your row, quilt a line about ¼" below the bottom of the pearls, mirroring the curves of the chain. When you get back to the left side of your practice square, quilt another chain of pearls, butting them against each other and against the wiggly line you just created. See how different that chain of pearls looks? You can vary this design in many ways.

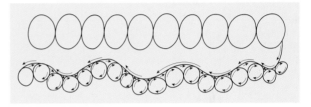

5. Fill the space below the wiggly chain of pearls with an allover pebble design. Start by making a single ½" circle, and then immediately make another one, and then another, continuing to build the design on itself and fill the space with pebbles. Stitch around each pebble as far as needed to get where you want to make your next pebble. If you find you've boxed yourself in, quilt over the existing lines of stitching, between the pebbles, until you reach open space, and then keep filling up the space.

6. Once you've quilted half of the bottom of your practice square, change up the scale of the pebbles and quilt much larger ones. Try varying the pebble size from ½" to 1", and even to 1½". See how much more realistic the pebbles look when they're not all the same size? The larger scale helps the quilting go faster, as you may have noticed. And as an added benefit, the

project will be softer and have a nicer drape than a piece with lots of tiny, closely spaced pebbles, which can feel somewhat stiff from all the dense quilting.

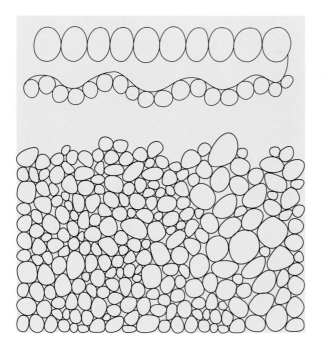

7. It may seem silly to practice drawing pebbling, as surely you are already proficient at drawing circles. But when you practice drawing them, the key is to not let your pen leave the paper. Instead, draw directly on top of existing lines to travel around the pebbles and to move to the next area to draw. All that practice will really help you become more comfortable quilting pebbles. So, get out that sketchbook and fill lots of pages with chains of pearls and pebbles. Make sure to vary the scale, drawing chains that are both straight and wiggly.

8. Quilt another practice square and compare it to your first attempt. Don't stress if your pebbles don't look perfect; just keep practicing them. Be sure to go very slowly when quilting pebbles and stay relaxed—it will really improve your results.

Tension Dilemmas

How is your thread tension looking? If you're having any problems at all with your tension for free-motion quilting, they'll surely show up while quilting pebbles. The nature of the design seems to aggravate any tension problems, so if your pebbles look tight or scrunched up, or if you can see a star of thread on the back because the front is pulling too tight—or vice versa—relax. Breathe. Test the tension as described on pages 17 and 18, but this time quilt a chain of pearls on your practice square. Once you get the tension dialed in just right, remember to write down the brand and weight of thread you are using and the tension setting that worked best for that thread.

Color Block Zip Bag

Pieced and quilted by Molly Hanson

FINISHED SIZE
9" x 5" x 4" deep

MATERIALS
Yardage is based on 42"-wide fabric.

1 piece, 9½" x 10½", *each of pink solid and yellow solid for bag*

2 pieces, 10" x 11", of fabric for lining

2 pieces, 10" x 11", of batting

2 squares, 2" x 2", of fabric to match zipper

10" all-purpose polyester zipper to match 1 of the bag fabrics

I'm a zip-bag collector; I use them for just about everything. I love making them and I love using them even more; they help me stay organized. And they make great gifts!

Because they're padded with batting and lining, quilted zip bags do a better job protecting their contents than plain lined ones. And here's a secret: they're actually easier—yes, easier—to make than regular zip bags. They're constructed so that the lining is the quilt backing, which means you skip several of the steps you'd do for a traditional lined bag.

This project is just the right size for makeup or other smaller items, but once you learn the process you can easily adapt the dimensions to make whatever size and shape you like.

INSTRUCTIONS

1. Layer the yellow rectangle on top of the pink rectangle and align the edges. Mark 2" down from the upper-left corner as shown. Mark 2" up from the lower-right corner. Align the edge of a ruler with the marks, and cut along the ruler's edge through both layers.

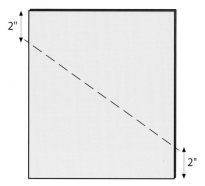

2. Rearrange the pieces so each block has two different colors. Sew the top pink and yellow pieces together to make a two-color block. Press the seam allowances open. Make a second two-color block as shown.

3. Layer each two-color block with batting and a lining piece; baste using your preferred method.

4. Quilt as shown in the quilting map.

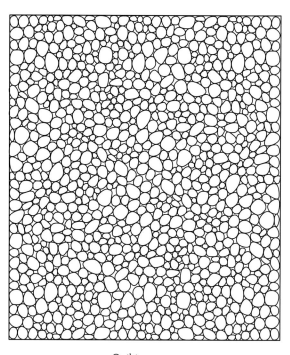

Quilting map

5. Trim the edges of the batting and backing even with the edges of the blocks. Zigzag stitch around the edges of both quilted blocks.

6. Press the zipper flat. Press each 2" square in half, wrong sides together. Align the raw edges of one folded square with one short end of the zipper. Sew the square in place using a ½" seam allowance. Flip the square open and press. In the same way, sew the remaining square to the other end of the zipper and press. Trim the squares even with the long sides of the zipper.

7. Place a quilted block on a flat surface, right side up with the pink edge at the top. With the zipper closed and wrong side up, place the zipper at the top of the block, aligning the top edges. Referring to "Zippers" on page 93, sew the zipper to the block. Press and topstitch ⅛" from the seam.

8. Repeat to sew the pink edge of the remaining quilted block on the opposite side of the zipper, making sure the sides of the blocks are aligned.

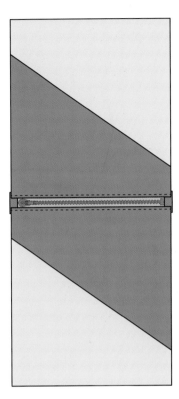

9. Unzip the zipper a little over halfway. (You will be turning the bag inside out through the open zipper.) With lining side facing out, align the raw edges along the sides and bottom and pin in place. Start ¼" from the zipper with a backstitch, sew around the side and bottom edges, stopping ¼" from the zipper with a backstitch.

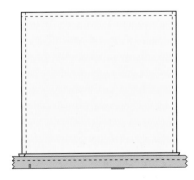

10. To make box-pleat corners, mark 2" in and down from each bottom corner as shown. Cut out the square from each corner, cutting on the marked line.

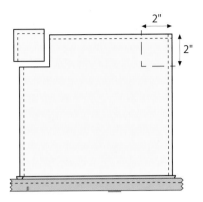

11. On one corner, place the bottom seam on top of the side seam. Pin the raw edges together. Sew the seam using a ¼" seam allowance. Then zigzag stitch over the raw edges so they won't fray. Repeat to box pleat the other bottom corner.

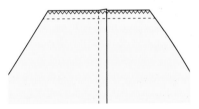

Join.

12. Turn the bag right side out, pushing out the zipper end corners and boxed corners. Using a scrap of fabric or ribbon, add a zipper pull to finish.

Color Block Toiletry Tote

Pieced and quilted by Molly Hanson

This is my favorite type of zip bag to make. I love the boxy shape and all the function that goes with it, and that side handle for quick grabbing? Love it! This bag also makes an impressive gift. Stock it with some fun bath goodies and you have a gift that either a guy or gal would love. Scale it down and you have a topnotch pencil case. Fill it with markers or colored pencils, add a sketchbook, and you have a great gift for any budding artist. Have I sold you yet? Let's give it a go!

FINISHED SIZE
10" x 6" x 4" deep

MATERIALS
Yardage is based on 42"-wide fabric.

1 piece, 11½" x 15½", each of yellow solid and blue solid for outer bag

2 pieces, 12" x 16", of fabric for lining

1 piece, 4" x 8", of yellow solid for handle

1 piece, 2½" x 4", of yellow solid for pull tab

2 pieces, 12" x 16", of fusible fleece

1 piece, 2" x 8", of fusible fleece

14" all-purpose polyester zipper to match 1 bag fabric

INSTRUCTIONS

1. Layer the yellow rectangle on top of the blue rectangle and align the edges. Mark 2" down from the upper-left corner as shown. Mark 2" up from the lower-right corner. Align the edge of a ruler with the marks, and cut along the ruler's edge through both layers.

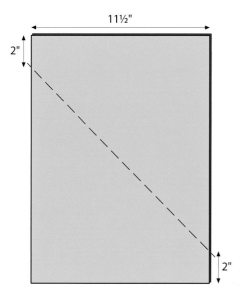

2. Rearrange the pieces on the top half so the blue piece is on top. Sew the top blue and yellow pieces together to make a two-color block. Press the seam allowances open. Make a second two-color block.

3. Following the manufacturer's instructions, fuse a 12" x 16" piece of fleece to the wrong side of a two-color block. Spray baste the other side of the fleece and layer with a lining piece. Repeat to baste the second two-color block, fleece, and lining piece together.

4. Quilt as shown in the quilting map.

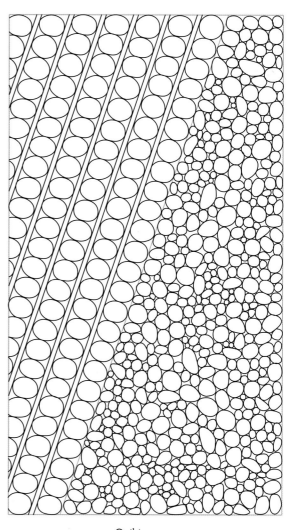

Quilting map

5. Trim and square up the quilted blocks to measure 10½" x 14½". Zigzag stitch around the edges of both quilted blocks.

6. To make the handles, press the yellow 4" x 8" piece in half lengthwise. Unfold the yellow piece and fuse the 2" x 8" piece of fleece in the center of the yellow piece using the crease as a guide. Fold the long sides of the yellow piece over the fleece, and then fold in half again along the first crease. Press again. Stitch ⅛" from both folded edges. Line up the edge of the presser foot with a previously stitched line and sew a few more lines of stitches.

7. Fold the yellow 2½" x 4" piece in half lengthwise, wrong sides together. Unfold and then fold the raw edges of the piece to the center crease and press. Refold on the center crease and press. Fold the piece in half to make

a ⅝" x 2" zipper tab. Stitch ⅛" from the folded edges. Place the tab on one end of the zipper as shown. Pin and topstitch across the tab about ⅛" from the folded edge.

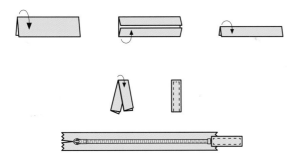

8. Place a quilted block on a flat surface, right side up with a yellow 14½"-long edge at the top. With the zipper closed and wrong side up, place the zipper at the top of the block, aligning the top edges. Referring to "Zippers" on page 93, sew the zipper to the block. Press and topstitch ⅛" from the seam.

9. Repeat to sew the yellow edge of the remaining quilted block on the opposite side of the zipper, making sure the sides of the blocks are aligned.

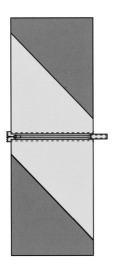

10. Unzip the zipper a little over halfway. (You will be turning the bag inside out through the open zipper.) With the lining side facing out, align the raw edges along the sides and bottom and pin in place. Sew along the bottom edge of the bag, using a ¼" seam allowance.

11. Place the bottom seam on top of the zipper and sew along both sides of the bag.

12. To make box-pleat corners, mark 2" in and 2" down from each corner. Cut out the square from each corner.

13. On one corner, pin the raw edges together. Sew the seam using a ¼" seam allowance. Then zigzag stitch over the raw edges so they won't fray. Repeat to box pleat the other corner on the same end of the bag.

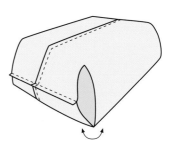

14. On the other end of the bag, insert the handle as shown. Align the raw edges and sew them together, making sure to catch the handle in the seam. Repeat the process on the last corner, making sure the other end of the handle is caught in the seam.

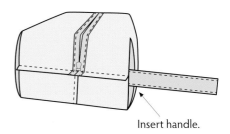

Insert handle.

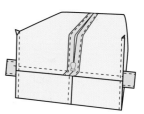

15. Turn the bag right side out and push out all of the corners.

Square Meander

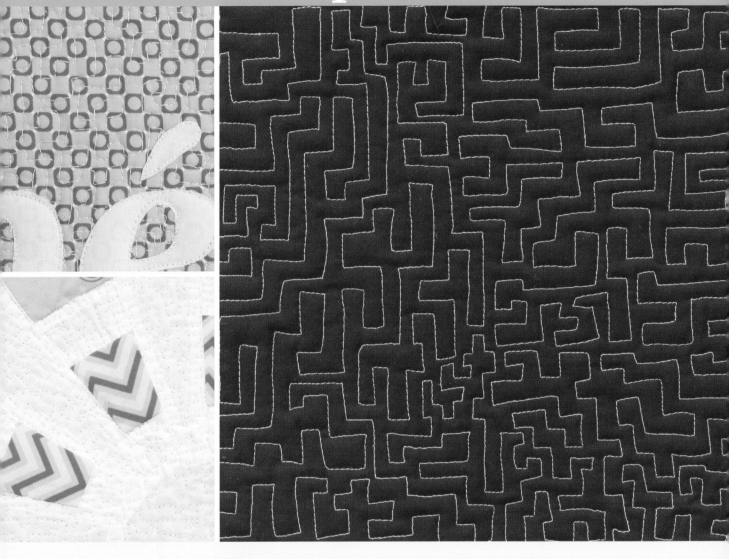

The square meander is a form of stippling. This design works well for masculine projects and lends a modern edge to any project. And just as with regular stippling, there are two key rules to follow when stitching this design. The first and most important is that you don't want to cross over your previous stitched lines. Proper stippling in any form has no crossed or intersecting lines. To avoid crossing previously stitched lines, you need to think about where you have already quilted and plan where you are going next. The second rule is to quilt right angles—think crossword puzzles or the video game Tetris. You want a blocky, angular look.

Following these two rules and filling the spaces consistently and evenly are all that you need to concern yourself with for this design. I recommend filling several pages of your sketchbook with drawings of square meander before attempting to stitch it. Try following the lines on graph paper as a guide the first few times. If you don't have sharp, 90° angles or your lines are a bit wavy, don't worry. This design will come much more easily to some people than to others. Personally, I'm much better at stitching fluid, wavy designs, so this isn't the easiest design for me. However, I love the look of the design, so I continue to practice it. And with practice I've improved. So will you!

INSTRUCTIONS

1. Set up your machine following "Five Prep Steps for Free-Motion Quilting" on page 21, and prepare a practice square.

2. Making sure your hands are in the proper position for maximum fabric control, slowly sew five or six stitches in place before stitching a 1" straight line to the right. Sew a few stitches in place (this helps keep the corners sharp instead of rounded), and then stitch a ½" straight line downward. Pause to sew a few stitches in place, and then stitch a ½" straight line to the right as shown.

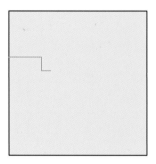

3. Sew a few stitches in place again and then stitch straight up 1". Sew a few stitches in place before stitching 1" to the left. Sew a few stitches in place, and then stitch upward ½".

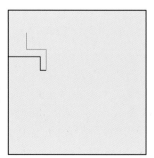

4. In the same way, stitch ½" to the left, stitch up ½", and then stitch 1" to the right, making sure to sew a few stitches in place at each corner.

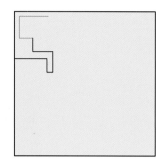

5. Continue as before, using ½" as your scale and making movements that feel nearly robotic. Stop to sew a few stitches at each corner and check every so often to make sure you're filling up the space consistently.

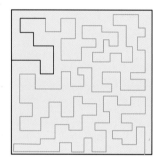

Practice Makes Perfect

Fill up your practice square, and then take a good look at it. What parts are going well and what aren't? Is it easier for you to stitch in some directions than others? Consider making adjustments to your quilting map so next time you can move your quilted piece in directions that make the stitching easier for you to do. Also, consider filling several more pages of your sketchbook with square meander drawings. When your drawings look good, and they are consistent and fairly easy to do without much thinking or stopping and starting, then prepare another practice square and give it another go. Marvel at how different the first and second squares look; see how much drawing makes a difference? "Chipped Plates Place Mats" (page 48) uses this style of quilting along with the next type of stitching, nesting boxes on page 45. Now you're ready to learn nesting boxes!

Nesting boxes is a fun and easy design that I've adapted from several different variations of box-in-box designs. This design is fairly simple to execute and looks great in borders. You can also use it as background fill when you want a more angular, modern look. This quilting design is referred to as an edge-to-edge design, and I used it in "Chipped Plates Place Mats" (page 48) as a background fill. It's a bit trickier using it in the background than as a border fill, because you don't necessarily have straight lines to follow to keep things angular and aligned. If keeping your stitching straight and perfect is important to you, you can mark lines at 2" intervals to guide you. As always, sketching the design over and over will really help with your quilting. With this design, I always stitch from left to right and then stitch across the bottom line of the just-stitched row to get back to the left and start a new row.

Travel Stitching

For this design, you'll need to travel stitch, which essentially means you'll have to quilt on top of previously quilted lines to move from one area to the next. Travel stitching is definitely worth practicing. It's an essential skill for free-motion quilting and will improve with much practice.

Travel stitching, like stitching in the ditch, is best done very slowly and carefully. Sew at a snail's pace and you'll find it isn't too hard at all. Don't forget to slow down your hands as well as your machine speed so they move in sync with one another. When you start, try not to focus on making every line straight, but instead try to master the slow-paced travel stitching and get the feel of moving from left to right in a set direction. Even with wonky lines this design looks great and modern and fun. So take it easy, sketch it lots, and have fun with it!

INSTRUCTIONS

1. Set up your machine following "Five Prep Steps for Free-Motion Quilting" on page 21, and prepare a practice square.

2. Before practicing this design, it's essential to properly prepare your practice square. This design is built off of "foundation walls," so defining an area to stitch is necessary. To create the stitching area, mark a line about 1" from each edge of your practice square, then stitch over the marked lines to create a stitched square. If desired, you can also mark a 2" grid inside the square you just created, which will make it easier to stitch the design evenly.

3. Starting 2" down from the upper-left corner of your square, stitch 2" to the right, pause to sew a few stitches in place to lock in the corner, and then stitch 2" upward to form a square.

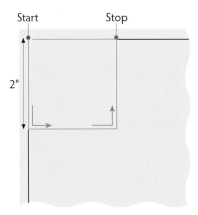

4. Travel stitch over the stitched line at the top of the square to get back to the far-left corner. Go slowly and take your time. In the far-left corner, sew a few stitches in place before stitching down ½" on the left side of the box. Sew a few stitches in place, stitch ½" to the right, and then sew a few stitches in place before stitching upward to close the square.

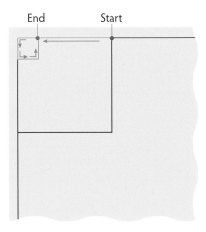

5. Travel stitch across the top stitching line toward the left corner, sew a few stitches in place, and stitch down 1" on the left side of the box. Sew a few stitches in place, stitch 1" to the right, and then sew a few stitches in place before stitching upward 1" to close the square. In the same way, travel stitch across the top and then down the left side 1½". Stitch 1½" to the right and then upward to close the square, making sure to sew a few stitches in place at each corner.

6. Continue in this manner, filling in 2" squares on your practice square. You can start in any corner, keep it consistent or change it up.

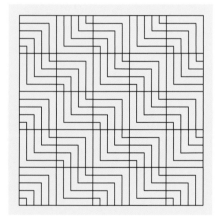

7. Look at your practice square and study the strong and weak areas. Is it easy for you to maintain the scale in this design? Would additional markings be helpful to get things started for you?

8. Sketch this design as many times as possible, making sure to never let the pen tip leave the paper, just like when stitching. Graph paper will make sketching this design much easier at first; however, after you have mastered it on graph paper, be sure to practice on plain paper too. That way you will start gaining the proper muscle memory with graph paper, and then challenge that muscle memory on plain paper before finally quilting the design on another practice square. Don't forget to compare the second square to the first one and take note of your improvements.

Varying Your Approach

Try drawing and quilting this design both with a marked grid and without. The free-form look of the design quilted without a marked grid lends a unique, more organic feeling to your project, while the marked version looks much more modern.

Chipped Plates Place Mats

Pieced and quilted by Molly Hanson

I have always loved the Dresden Plate quilt pattern. It's such a classic design with so many options for making it your own. I wanted my version of the Dresden Plate to look like modern dinnerware and I think I achieved that. I also think the little chip detail makes the design a bit more whimsical and fun. Are you ready to make your own set of chipped plate place mats?

FINISHED SIZE
12" x 18"

MATERIALS
Yardage is based on 42"-wide fabric and is sufficient for 2 place mats.

½ yard of red print for background

½ yard of white solid for Dresden Plate

½ yard of pink polka dot for Dresden Plate and binding

⅛ yard of pink zigzag print for Dresden Plate

½ yard of fabric for backing

14" x 40" piece of batting

½ yard of paper-backed fusible web

Template plastic

Optional: Easy Dresden ruler by Darlene Zimmerman (or any Dresden Plate ruler that cuts 20 petals to make a full circle)

CUTTING

From the red print, cut:
2 rectangles, 12½" x 18½"

From the pink polka dot, cut:
1 strip, 2" x 42"
4 strips, 2½" x 42"

From the pink zigzag print, cut:
1 strip, 2" x 42"

From the white solid, cut:
3 strips, 1½" x 42"
1 strip, 6½" x 42"

From the backing fabric, cut:
2 pieces, 14" x 20"

From the batting, cut:
2 pieces, 14" x 20"

INSTRUCTIONS

1. Using the white 1½"-wide strips, pink polka-dot 2" strip, and pink zigzag strip, join the strips along their long edges to make a strip set. Gently press the seam allowances open to reduce the bulk.

2. Use the pattern on page 50 and template plastic to make a petal template. Use the template or the 6½" line on a Dresden ruler to cut 10 petals from the strip set, rotating the template or ruler after each cut as shown. (If the ruler doesn't have a 6½" line, measure 6½" from the bottom of the ruler and mark the spot with masking tape.) Separate the petals into two stacks of five matching petals. One stack will have a pink polka-dot strip at the top and the other stack will have a pink zigzag strip at the top.

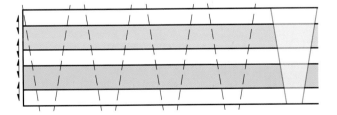

3. Cut 10 petals from the white 6½"-wide strip, rotating the template or ruler after each cut.

4. Lay out one set of strip-set petals and five white petals, alternating them as shown. Sew the petals together to make a half plate, making sure to line up the top edges of the petals. Don't worry about the bottom edge, as it will be covered later with the center circle. Carefully press the seam allowances open.

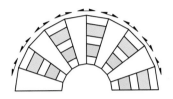

5. Following the manufacturer's instructions, apply fusible web to the wrong side of the half plate. Position the half plate on one long edge of a red rectangle, aligning the raw edges. Cut a chip from the plate. Then fuse the plate in place. Fuse the chip in place, about ½" from its original spot.

6. Repeat steps 4 and 5 to make a second place-mat top.

7. Using the pattern on page 50, trace a circle onto the paper side of the fusible web. Fuse the circle onto a scrap of white solid and cut out the circle. Then cut the circle in half. On each place-mat top, place a half circle at the base of the petals, covering the raw edges, and fuse in place.

8. Topstitch ⅛" from the outer edges of the plate and the center circle. Or, use a zigzag or buttonhole stitch to secure the appliqués.

9. Layer each place-mat top with batting and backing; baste using your preferred method. I like to spray baste small projects. Refer to "Basting" on page 13 as needed.

10. Using nesting boxes and square meander designs, quilt each place mat as shown in the quilting map. You can start or stop anywhere.

Quilting map

11. Trim the batting and backing even with the place-mat top. Referring to "Binding" on page 94, use the pink polka-dot 2½"-wide strips to bind the edges.

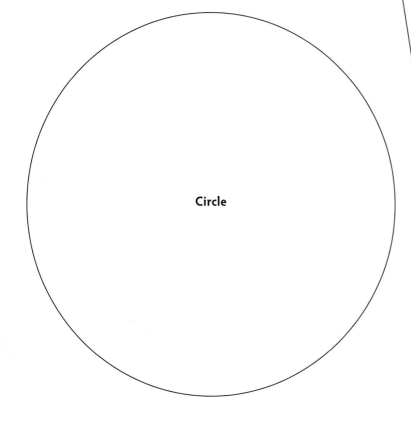

¼" seam allowance

Dresden petal

Straight of grain

Circle

Circle pattern does not include seam allowance.

Bon Appétit Table Runner

Appliquéd and quilted by Molly Hanson

FINISHED SIZE
15½" x 40"

MATERIALS
Yardage is based on 42"-wide fabric. A fat quarter measures 18" x 21".

½ yard of red print for background

1 fat quarter of white solid for appliquéd letters

¼ yard of pink zigzag print for binding

½ yard of pink print for backing

17½" x 42" piece of batting

½ yard of paper-backed fusible web

Nothing complements a new set of place mats like a fresh new table runner. While designing this table runner, I thought of my guy's aunt Janine. I associate her with amazing food, as she has served some of the best I've ever had the pleasure of tasting. Janine lives in Belgium and speaks French. Every time we sit down to eat, she says "Bon appétit," with a sparkle in her eye. She is passionate about feeding people; it's how she shows her love. I think I'll give her this table runner, since quilted items are my passion and giving them to friends and family is how I show my love!

CUTTING

From the red print, cut:
1 strip, 15½" x 40"

From the pink print, cut:
1 piece, 17½" x 42"

From the pink zigzag print, cut:
3 strips, 2½" x 42"

APPLIQUÉ LETTERS

I created the letters on my computer using Microsoft Word. I selected the Georgia font in a 320-point size (you have to manually enter 320), and then selected Italic. Once I had the font set, I typed the phrase I planned to use. Before printing, choose the landscape orientation to print several letters on each page.

1. Print the letters onto plain white paper and carefully cut them out. Take your time and go slowly; neatness makes all the difference in raw-edge appliqué.

2. Lay out the letters on the white solid to determine how much fabric you will need to use. Following the manufacturer's instructions, apply fusible web to the wrong side of the white solid, covering the predetermined area. Do not remove the paper.

3. Lightly spray a coating of basting spray over the back of all the paper letters and adhere them to the right side of the fused white solid. If you don't want to use basting spray, flip the paper letters over so the printed side is facing down and the letters are reversed. Then trace the letters onto the paper side of the fused fabric.

4. Cut out the letters and remove the paper backing.

ASSEMBLY

1. Fold the red strip in half vertically and then horizontally. Gently press along the fold lines to establish centering lines. Center the letters on the red strip and fuse them in place.

2. Layer the table-runner top with batting and backing; baste using your preferred method. I like to spray baste small projects. Refer to "Basting" on page 13 as needed.

3. Quilt the table runner as shown in the quilting map below. You can start and stop anywhere.

4. Trim the batting and backing even with the table-runner top. Referring to "Binding" on page 94, use the zigzag-print 2½"-wide strips to bind the edges.

Quilting map

Paisley

Paisley is a classical design with ancient roots. It originated in Persia and became popular by way of Persian rugs flooding the European markets. Featured on everything from silk scarves and neckties to ancient tapestries and rugs, a design with that kind of staying power is surely a good one to know! Paisley quilting is created by layering basic teardrop shapes and nestling many of them together to cover an area. I find this design very relaxing to quilt or draw. I like the challenge of fitting paisleys together like puzzle pieces. You can quilt over previous lines of stitching to move from one area to another, so it's very forgiving. Paisley is also a fun design to highlight and enhance as a motif, which I demonstrate in "Purple Paisley Tote Bag" on page 55.

INSTRUCTIONS

1. Set up your machine following "Five Prep Steps for Free-Motion Quilting" on page 21, and prepare a practice square.

2. Making sure your hands are in the proper position for maximum fabric control, sew five or six stitches in place before slowly stitching a 1"-long teardrop.

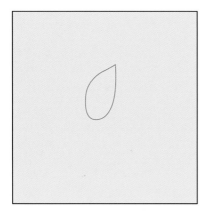

3. When you get back to where you started, immediately start forming a 1½"-long teardrop.

4. Back at the starting point, quilt a smaller paisley to the right of the one you just stitched, leaving a small space between the shapes for the larger paisley. Stitch a larger paisley around the small paisley, taking care to stitch right next to or on top of the stitching lines of the previous paisley.

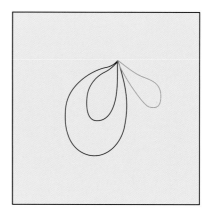

5. In the same manner, quilt a small and then large paisley between the first two paisleys as shown.

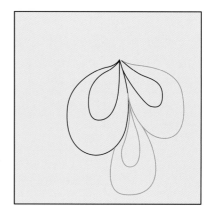

6. Continue stitching teardrop shapes in all directions to fill the space. Varying the size is typical, but try to keep them the same relative scale (not smaller than ½" or larger than 2½").

Paisley and Angles

When learning free-motion quilting, one skill that some find easier than others is deciding what design to use. I've always enjoyed choosing designs and I like sketching the designs on top of blocks so I can visualize the outcome. In my sketching and quilting, I have come to realize that paisley designs always look great in blocks with lots of triangles. It's easy to start the design in a corner and work your way out—so angles and paisley work well together. Next time you're choosing a design for a quilt block with lots of triangles, consider paisley!

Purple Paisley Tote Bag

Pieced and quilted by Molly Hanson

FINISHED SIZE
15" x 18"

MATERIALS
Yardage is based on 42"-wide fabric. A fat quarter measures 18" x 21".

15 strips, 3½" x 21", of assorted purple solids for outer bag

½ yard of fabric for lining

1 fat quarter of dark-purple solid for strap and binding

2 pieces, 16" x 19", of fusible fleece

1 piece, 2" x 21", of fusible fleece

One can never have too many tote bags, especially quilted ones with their built-in padding. This tote is the perfect size for books or a laptop. I made one for myself a few years ago and it's still the first bag I grab. Plus, carrying a bag you made gives you an excellent opportunity to share your love of quilting with the world. This bag uses 15 different shades of purple (why not, right?). You could use as few as two colors or all scraps and still create a great effect. As long as you can practice quilting on it you can't go wrong!

INSTRUCTIONS

1. Randomly join three purple strips along their long edges as shown to make a strip set. Press the seam allowances in one direction. Make five strip sets. Cut four 3½"-wide segments from each strip set.

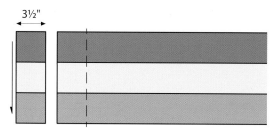

Make 5 strip sets.
Cut 4 segments from each strip set (20 total).

2. Lay out five assorted segments from step 1 as desired. Join the segments to make a rectangular unit. Press the seam allowances in one direction. Make a total of four units.

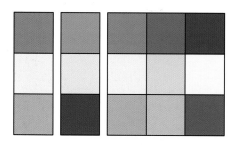

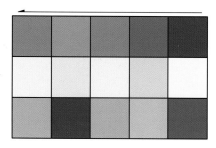

Make 4.

3. Sew two units from step 2 together to make the bag front. Press the seam allowances in one direction. Repeat to make the bag back.

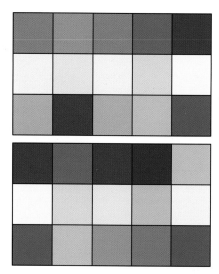

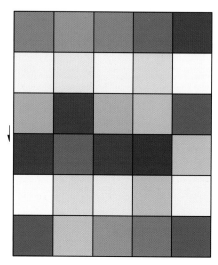

Make 2.

4. Center and fuse a 16" x 19" piece of fleece to the wrong side of the bag front and the bag back.

5. Cut the lining fabric into two 17" x 20" pieces. Spray baste one lining piece to the fleece side of the bag front. Spray baste the other lining piece to the fleece side of the bag back.

6. Quilt the bag front as shown in the quilting map. Quilt the bag back using the same design or a simpler paisley motif.

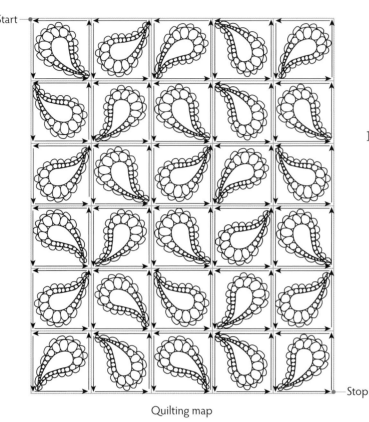

Quilting map

7. Trim the lining and fleece even with the edges of the bag front and back. Zigzag stitch the sides and bottom edges of the bag front and bag back.

8. From the dark-purple, cut two 2½" x 21" strips. Use the strips to bind the top edge of the bag front and bag back, referring to "Binding" on page 94 as needed.

9. With right sides together, pin the bag front and back pieces together, matching the seam intersections. Using a generous ¼" seam allowance, sew along the sides and bottom of the bag, making sure to start and stop with a backstitch. Turn the bag right side out.

10. From the remaining dark purple, cut a 5" x 21" strip. On the wrong side of the strip, fuse the 2" x 21" piece of fleece along one edge of the dark-purple strip. Wrap the dark-purple strip around the fleece, covering both long edges. Then fold the raw edge under and topstitch along the folded edge. Using the edge of the presser foot as a guide, stitch several straight vertical lines ¼" apart through the strap. This makes a very sturdy and comfortable strap.

11. On the outside of the bag, place one end of the strap on top of the side seam, aligning the raw edges of the strap with the bottom edge of the binding. Pin and sew the strap in place as shown. Flip the strap up, covering the raw edges, and stitch it in place. In the same way, sew the strap to the other side of the bag.

Stitch.

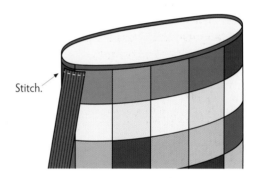

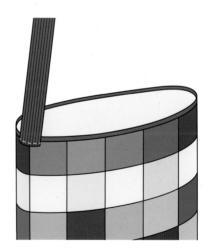

Quilt Block Pillow

Pieced and quilted by Molly Hanson

Sometimes the scariest part of quilting a beautifully pieced quilt is simply starting. Once you start quilting the last thing you want to do is rip out the stitches. But getting over the fear may be easier than you think. When I first started free-motion quilting, I made an extra block from each quilt to use as a practice square before starting on the actual quilt, and then turned the quilted block into a matching pillow for the quilt. I've done this with every quilt since; the practice builds confidence and gives me a chance to work out ideas. Here, I chose a Pinwheel block because it looks so nice with paisley quilting.

FINISHED SIZE
16" x 16"

MATERIALS
Yardage is based on 42"-wide fabric. Fat quarters measure 18" x 21".

1 fat quarter *each* of gray solid and blue solid for pillow front

1 fat quarter of coordinating print for pillow back

17" x 17" square of fabric for pillow-front backing

17" x 17" square of batting

16" x 16" pillow form

CUTTING

All strips are cut across the lengthwise grain, parallel to the selvage.

From the gray solid, cut:
   1 strip, 5½" x 18"; crosscut into 2 squares, 5½" x 5½"
   2 strips, 3½" x 9½"
   2 strips, 3½" x 16½"

From the blue solid, cut:
   1 strip, 5½" x 18"; crosscut into 2 squares, 5½" x 5½"
   5 strips, 2½" x 18"

From the coordinating print, cut:
   2 rectangles, 10½" x 16½"

INSTRUCTIONS

1. Draw a diagonal line from corner to corner on the wrong side of each gray square. Layer a gray square right sides together with a blue square. Sew ¼" from each side of the marked line. Cut the squares apart on the drawn line to make two half-square-triangle units. Press the seam allowances toward the blue triangles. Trim the units to measure 4½" square. Repeat to make a total of four units.

  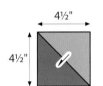

Make 4.

2. Arrange the half-square-triangle units in two rows as shown. Sew the units together in rows. Press the seam allowances in the directions indicated. Join the rows and press the seam allowances in one direction. The block should measure 9½" x 9½".

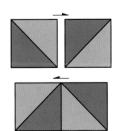 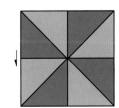

3. Sew gray 3½" x 9½" strips to opposite sides of the block. Press the seam allowances open. Sew gray 3½" x 16½" strips to the top and bottom of the block. Press the seam allowances open.

4. Layer the block with batting and backing; baste using your preferred method. Quilt as shown in the quilting map, following the general direction of the blue arrows.

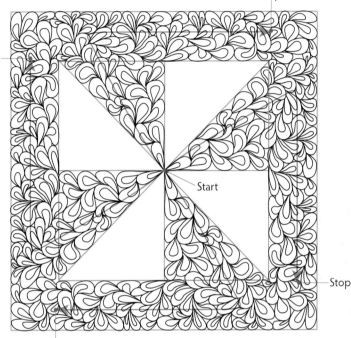

Quilting map

5. Trim the batting and backing even with the edges of the block to complete the pillow front.

6. To make the pillow back, fold over ¼" on one 16½" edge of both print rectangles and press. Fold over ¼" again and press. Machine stitch along the folded edge.

Directional Print

If your pillow back has a directional print, position the two print rectangles side by side, making sure the print is facing in the same direction on both rectangles. Fold and stitch the edges that are next to each other as described in step 6.

7. Overlap the pillow backs on top of the pillow front, *wrong* sides together, as shown. Machine baste around the pillow using a scant ¼" seam allowance. Remove the pins and trim the pillow back even with the pillow front, if needed.

Overlap

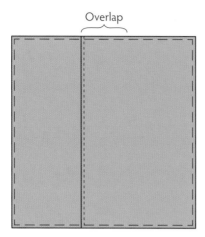

8. Referring to "Binding" on page 94, use the blue 2½"-wide strips to bind the edges of the pillow. Insert the pillow form through the opening.

Wood Grain

Quilting designs based on nature always seem to find their way into the inner depths of my heart. I'm a girl who would rather be fishing than shopping, and the outdoors beckon me, offering artistic inspiration as well as peace and tranquility. Quilting nature-based designs seems to bring me that same sense of calm. Wood grain is a design that relies on imperfection for its beauty. This is not a design to stress out about or fuss over. Small wiggles and bumps give it character, and variance in width of the grain adds to the beauty. It's hard to make this design look bad! When I was first learning to quilt, I found much success with wood grain, along with a boost in my confidence when I discovered I could achieve something beautiful. Hopefully this design will lead you to a place of tranquility, while elevating your quilting confidence as well!

INSTRUCTIONS

1. Set up your machine following "Five Prep Steps for Free-Motion Quilting" on page 21, and prepare a practice square.

2. Making sure your hands are in the proper position for maximum fabric control, sew five or six stitches in place before slowly stitching a wiggly line, from left to right, across your practice square.

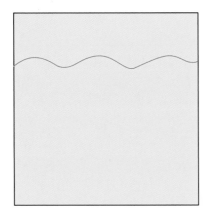

3. When you get to the edge of the practice square, stitch down approximately ¼" and echo the same wiggly path, stitching from right to left. About halfway across the square, stop at the base of a wiggle to quilt a "knot" in the wood. Quilt an arc, and then quilt an arc beneath the first arc to create an eye shape. Stop stitching ½" before you get to the start of your knot.

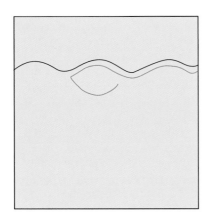

4. Quilt a smaller arc ½" below the first arc, stopping ½" from the left corner of the knot, and then quilt the lower arc. Stop stitching ½"

from the right corner of the knot. Make a small hook shape in the center.

5. Starting in the center, stitch between the lines you just quilted to spiral back out of the knot. When you reach the starting point underneath the knot, continue stitching the wiggly line toward the left side of the square to finish the row.

6. Continue stitching rows and adding a knot every couple of rows. Be sure to scatter the knots so they look natural.

Use in Manageable Spaces

Wood grain is an edge-to-edge design, which means you'll be working from one edge of your quilting area to the opposite edge. If you attempt to quilt wood grain across a huge quilt surface, you will have to constantly move the entire quilt back and forth to create the design. That's an awful lot of work! It is best to choose specific, manageable areas of your quilt for this design, or quilt it across the entire surface of smaller items.

Hardwood Messenger Bag

Pieced and quilted by Molly Hanson

FINISHED SIZE
15" x 12" x 3" deep

MATERIALS
Yardage is based on 42"-wide fabric. A fat quarter measures 18" x 21".

8 strips, 3½" x 24", of assorted wood-colored (tan, brown, cream, taupe, gray) solids for outer bag (scraps work well, or try batiks)

½ yard of fabric for lining

1 fat quarter of coordinating fabric for side panels

½ yard of brown solid for strap and binding

27" x 36" piece of fusible fleece

All quilters share a love of giving handmade gifts, but not everyone is easy to make something for. Men can be especially difficult; many fabrics and quilting designs have a feminine look. Wood grain is one quilting design that works great for guys. When I set out to create a bag for a guy that would showcase wood-grain quilting, I envisioned a hardwood floor wrapped up into a messenger bag. Stitching in the ditch creates the look of planks and gives you small, individual areas to quilt, which makes it so much easier. I omitted pockets and kept the design simple so you could focus on the quilting.

CUTTING

From the assorted wood-colored solids for outer bag, cut a *total* of:
 8 strips, 3½" x 24"; crosscut into:
  12 rectangles, 3½" x 12"
  6 rectangles, 3½" x 6¼"

From the coordinating fabric for side panels, cut:
 4 rectangles, 3½" x 12"
 1 strip, 2" x 15½"

From the fabric for lining, cut:
 1 strip, 17" x 38"

From the fusible fleece, cut:
 1 strip, 15½" x 36"
 1 strip, 5" x 36"
 2 rectangles, 3½" x 12"

From the brown solid for strap and binding, cut:
 1 strip, 5½" x 36"
 4 strips, 2½" x 42"

INSTRUCTIONS

1. Sew the rectangles together in rows as shown in the diagram following step 2. Press the seam allowances open. Join the rows and press the seam allowances open. Trim the bag panel to measure 15½" x 34½".

2. Sew the 2" x 15½" strip to one end of the bag panel. Press the seam allowances toward the just-added strip. This is the top of the bag body. The bag body should measure 15½" x 36".

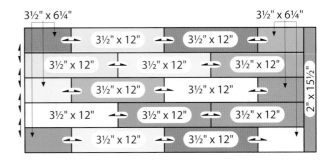

3. Following the manufacturer's instructions, fuse the fleece 15½"-wide strip to the wrong side of the bag body.

4. Spray baste the lining piece to the fleece side of the bag body.

5. Quilt the bag body as shown in the quilting map below. Trim the lining even with the edges of the bag body.

6. Fuse a fleece 3½" x 12" rectangle to the wrong side of a side-panel rectangle. Spray baste a side-panel rectangle to the other side of the fleece as the lining. Repeat the process with the remaining fleece rectangle and two side-panel rectangles. Using the edge of the presser foot as a guide, stitch straight lines ¼" apart down the middle of each side panel. Square up each side panel as needed.

Quilting map

7. Press one brown 2½"-wide strip in half lengthwise, wrong sides together. Referring to "Binding" on page 94, use the strip to bind one short end of each side panel and the top edge of the bag body.

8. Pin one side panel to the bag body, lining sides together, starting at the upper-right corner of the side panel as shown. At the corner of the side panel, gently ease the bag panel around the corner and pin to secure. Continue in the same way, pinning and easing around the other corner and then up the other side of the panel. Repeat the process, pinning the side panel to the other side of the bag panel.

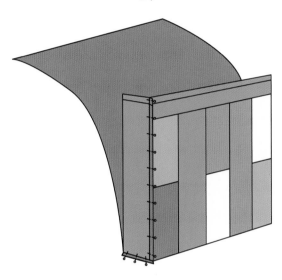

9. Using a scant ¼" seam allowance, sew the side panels to the bag body, removing the pins as you go and being careful to keep the pieces aligned at the corners. The seam will be on the outside of the bag and will be finished with binding.

10. Join the remaining three brown 2½"-wide strips to make a long strip. Press the strip in half lengthwise, wrong sides together. Leaving a 1" tail and starting at the upper-right corner of the bag body with a backstitch, sew the binding strip to the right side of the bag as shown, easing around the side-panel corners and mitering the 90° corners on the bag flap. When

you reach the upper-left corner of the bag, stop with a backstitch. Trim off the excess strip, leaving a 1" tail.

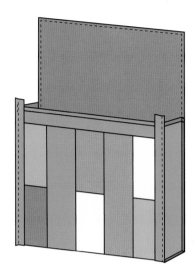

11. Fold the binding tails down, even with the top edge, and then fold the binding over the raw edges, covering the line of machine stitches. Machine stitch along the folded edge.

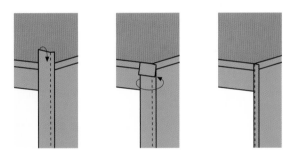

12. To make the strap, center and fuse the fleece 5"-wide strip on the wrong side of the brown 5½"-wide strip, making sure there is a ¼" seam allowance along both long edges. Then fold the strip in half lengthwise, right sides together, and stitch along the long raw edge. Turn the strap right side out. Press the tube flat, pressing the seam allowances to one side. Topstitch along both edges of the strap. Using the edge of the presser foot as a guide, stitch several straight lines ¼" apart vertically through the strap.

13. On the outside of the bag, center one end of the strap on a side panel, aligning the raw edges of the strap with the bottom edge of the binding. Pin and sew across the end of the strap. Flip the strap up, covering the raw edges, and stitch it in place. In the same way, sew the strap to the other side of the bag.

Outward Bound Laptop Sleeve

Made and quilted by Molly Hanson

These days we all have precious gadgets that need protection from bumps and scrapes. From smart phones to laptops, tablets, and media players, the technology that needs to be softly padded in quilty love is endless. This very simple media sleeve can be custom fitted to any device. I made this one to fit my laptop and added a heart and initials to make it look like someone had carved them in wood. Personalize your sleeve with initials, names, or messages inside the heart and then quilt Wood Grain around it. This project makes good use of practice squares of all sizes, and these sleeves make excellent gifts for the hard-to-make-for people in your life.

FINISHED SIZE
17" x 10½"

MATERIALS
Yardage is based on 42"-wide fabric.

¾ yard of rust solid for outer sleeve, sleeve lining, and binding

18" x 21" piece of batting

4"-long piece of ¼"-wide elastic

1 toggle button, ¾" long

CUTTING

From the rust solid, cut:
   2 pieces, 18" x 21"
   2 strips, 2½" x 42"

INSTRUCTIONS

1. Referring to "Spray Basting" on page 15, layer the two rust pieces with batting and spray baste the layers together.

2. Quilt as shown in the quilting map.

Quilting map

3. Lay your device on top of the quilted sleeve and fold the sleeve in half over the device, making sure the device is completely covered.

4. Referring to "Binding" on page 94 and using a rust 2½"-wide strip, bind both short edges of your sleeve.

5. Fold the sleeve in half again, right side facing out, and sew along one end, using a scant ¼" seam allowance.

6. Using a rust 2½"-wide strip and leaving a 1" tail at each end, sew the binding to the sleeve front on the just-sewn side. Fold the tails over the top and bottom edges, and then fold the binding over the raw edges, covering the line of machine stitches. Machine stitch along the folded edge.

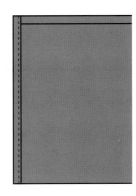

7. Slip the device into the sleeve, making sure it is nestled against the sewn side and bottom of the sleeve. On the open end, place a pin on the top and bottom edges where the next seam will go to securely contain the device. Remove the device and mark a line connecting the two pins. Place a few pins along the marked line. Insert and remove the device to make sure it is a good fit. Adjust the pins as necessary.

8. Sew along the marked line and trim the excess fabric, leaving a ¼" seam allowance.

9. Repeat step 6 to bind the just-sewn seam.

10. Fold the elastic in half to make a loop. On the back lining, center the loop just below the binding; sew the loop in place, making sure to backstitch several times to secure the loop. Insert the device in the sleeve. Gently pull the elastic loop over the top to see where it should lie for a secure fit. Making sure the loop is centered on the sleeve front, mark a dot inside the loop so you know where to sew the button. Sew the button in place.

Print Tracking

Print tracking is just what it sounds like—you pick all or part of a design in a printed fabric and quilt right on top of the design. This allows you to make the fabric design really stand out, while giving you the opportunity to quilt all sorts of new shapes you might not try otherwise. Print tracking also reinforces the same skills that travel stitching, stitching around appliqués, and stitching in the ditch require—that is, the ability to put that needle exactly where you intend it to go. This skill is one of the most important fundamentals of good free-motion quilting, so by practicing print tracking you are doing some excellent skill building.

To practice this technique, I recommend making a selection of practice squares. For the top fabric, use different types of prints such as simple geometric designs, large-scale florals, and simple novelty motifs. When choosing fabric, try to imagine how you'd quilt it. Would you pick just certain elements to highlight, or would you quilt every part of the print? How would you move around from place to place? Thinking this way during the selection process will help you when it's time to quilt. Starting with a plan is always a good idea when trying something new!

The best thing about print tracking is that it gives you a chance to highlight your favorite prints. Come on, we all started quilting because we are addicted to buying fabric, right? So, for the love of the fabric and the chance to build your free-motion quilting skills, let's practice print tracking.

INSTRUCTIONS

1. Set up your machine following "Five Prep Steps for Free-Motion Quilting" on page 21, and prepare a practice square.

2. Decide which part of the print you want to track. Starting on the edge of the square and making sure your hands are in the proper placement for maximum fabric control, sew five or six stitches in place before starting to quilt.

3. Focus on the edge of the print and, moving very slowly, start following the line. Instead of looking directly at the needle, look about ½" in front of the needle. Focusing on the needle is too distracting because of the movement, so think of driving, and how you look ahead at the road and horizon to stay in the middle of your lane. Looking just ahead of the needle works the same way.

4. Keep stitching around your print very slowly. Move the fabric as needed so you can quilt comfortably, and stop often to change the position of your hands.

5. Once you have tracked your print, you need to figure out how to move to the next part of the print you want to track. You have two options. You can stop, break the thread, and start over at the edge on another part of the print. On smaller projects this method isn't too much trouble, because you won't stop and start over very often. However, on big quilts stopping and starting can be really annoying, so I like to use a different method. Instead of breaking

the thread, I quilt a chain of pearls to connect the designs. This adds an interesting element to the fabric design and I avoid having to stop and break the thread. Either way works and I recommend trying both to see which you prefer.

A chain of pearls connects one floral design to the other.

6. Fill several practice squares with different types of print tracking. This is one time when lots of practice squares are required; drawing won't help with this technique. I suggest using practice squares that are big enough that they might be turned into one of the projects in the book—remember waste not, want not!

Coordinating Thread

Print tracking, while beautiful when done well, can look a little messy if you use contrasting thread and you wander outside the lines. Try using a thread that matches the background color of the fabric or blends really well, and stitch just outside the print—that way little mistakes won't be noticeable, but the texture will still make the print pop!

Good Boy Dog Bed

Made and quilted by Molly Hanson

As the dog mom of two gorgeous Labradoodles, I've made several dog beds over the years. My experiments have taught me a few things about the form and function—and durability—of a good dog bed. Quilted dog beds hold up very well and get softer with washing. You can use any quilted piece that is an appropriate size. If you don't have a dog in need of a new bed, why not make one as a gift or to donate to a local animal shelter? If all shelter pups had a comfy quilted bed, their world would be a little bit better. This design is simple while still offering good looks and functionality. I'll even show you how to avoid spending a penny for stuffing!

FINISHED SIZE

20" x 28", appropriate for a small-sized dog

See "Larger Dog Beds" on page 71, for alternate sizing.

MATERIALS

Yardage is based on 42"-wide fabric.

¾ yard of print for dog-bed top

¾ yard of fabric for lining

¾ yard of duck cloth or decorator fabric for dog-bed bottom

1 yard of fabric for insert (see "Options for Filling" on page 72)

¼ yard of fabric for binding

24" x 32" piece of batting

1 yard of 22"-wide heavyweight nonwoven fusible
  interfacing

Poly beads, polyester fiberfill, or shredded paper
  for filling

Larger Dog Beds

To make a bed for a medium-sized dog, you'll
need the following fabrics:

- 1 yard of print for dog-bed top
- 1 yard of fabric for lining
- 1¾ yards of duck cloth or decorator fabric
  for dog-bed bottom
- 2 yards of fabric for insert (see "Options
  for Filling" on page 72)
- ⅜ yard of fabric for binding
- 34" x 42" piece of batting
- 2 yards of 22"-wide heavyweight nonwoven
  fusible interfacing

Add 10" to each dimension in the cutting list.
You'll need 4 strips, 2½" x 42", for binding.

To make a bed for a large dog, you'll need the
following fabrics:

- 1⅝ yards of print for dog-bed top
- 1⅝ yards of fabric for lining
- 2⅜ yards of duck cloth or decorator fabric
  for dog-bed bottom
- 3 yards of fabric for insert (see "Options
  for Filling")
- ½ yard of fabric for binding
- 44" x 52" piece of batting
- 3 yards of 22"-wide heavyweight nonwoven
  fusible interfacing

Add 20" to each dimension in the cutting list.
You'll need 5 strips, 2½" x 42", for binding.

CUTTING

From the print for dog-bed top, cut:
  1 piece, 22" x 30"

From the fabric for lining, cut:
  1 piece, 24" x 32"

From the duck cloth or decorator fabric for dog-
bed bottom, cut:
  1 piece, 20" x 22"
  1 piece, 16" x 20"

From the fabric for insert, cut:
  2 pieces, 21" x 29"

From the fabric for binding, cut:
  3 strips, 2½" x 42"

From the interfacing, cut:
  1 piece, 22" x 30"

INSTRUCTIONS

1. Following the manufacturer's instruction, fuse
   the interfacing to the wrong side of the dog-
   bed top piece.

2. Layer the dog-bed top with batting and lining.
   Baste using your preferred method.

3. Quilt using print tracking. My fabric was printed
   with hexagons, so I used print tracking to quilt
   the lines as shown in the quilting map. Note
   that you may need to backtrack over some
   quilted lines to get to the next area of the print.

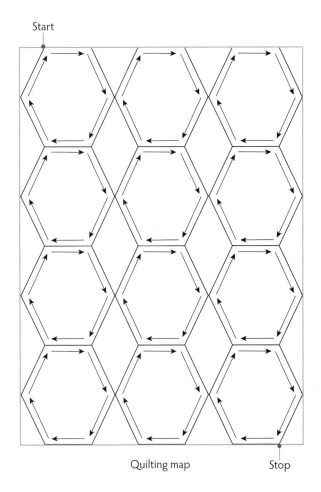

Quilting map

4. Trim the quilted piece to measure 20" x 28".

5. To make the bottom of the bed, fold over 1" on one 20" edge of both bottom pieces, and then fold over 1" again. Press and topstitch along the folded edges.

6. Place the two bottom pieces *wrong* side up on a flat surface, overlapping the folded edges about 6". Place the quilted piece on top of the bottom pieces, right side up. Pin around the edges, making sure the bottom pieces stay in place. Sew the pieces together using a ¼" seam allowance. Then sew ⅛" inside the seam allowance. This will add strength to the bed and help the edges lie flat for the binding.

7. Referring to "Binding" on page 94, use the 2½"-wide strips to bind the edges.

8. To make the insert, place the two pieces of insert fabric right sides together. Sew along three sides to make a pocket. Turn the pocket right side out. Fill the pocket with the stuffing material and then sew the open end closed. If you're using beads, be careful not to overfill; a little less than half full is perfect. If you're using fiberfill, overfilling a bit is recommended as the fiberfill tends to compress over time.

9. Slip the insert through the opening in the bottom of the bed.

Options for Filling

Below are several options for filling your dog bed. If you are filling the bed with poly beads or polyester fiberfill, you'll need to make an insert to hold the stuffing.

Poly beads (aka beanbag fill). The benefits are that it is soft, pliable, and dogs love it. It's very comfortable and nice looking. The disadvantage is that if you have a puppy or a dog that just generally likes to chew, this filling could be toxic to ingest, so it is best used only for mature, non-chewing dogs.

Polyester fiberfill. The benefit is that it is soft and pillow-like. The insert can be filled until firm for arthritic dogs and is washable. The disadvantage is that the filling compresses over time and may need refilling or replacing from time to time.

Shredded paper. Yes, if you have a paper shredder, don't throw that precious paper away. Save it up and stuff it into a heavy-duty trash bag. When the bag is full, tape it closed, and you have created a disposable and virtually free insert for a dog bed. This type of insert is temporarily comfortable and perfect for donating to the shelter, as it can be changed out and the dog bed can be washed and reused for another dog. It is great for puppies and incontinent senior dogs for the very same reason. The disadvantage is that the paper compresses rather quickly and will need changing several times a year to keep the bed soft and comfortable. Consider this option if you are making a bed to donate, but for a gift or for your own pet, one of the other fillings is preferable.

Makiko Ironing-Board Cover

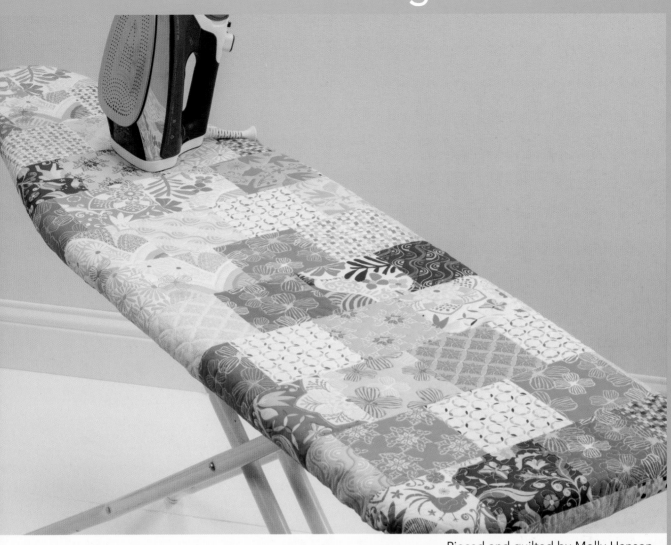

Pieced and quilted by Molly Hanson

FINISHED SIZE
60" x 20"

MATERIALS

Yardage is based on 42"-wide fabric.

79 squares, 5" x 5", of assorted prints for top

2½ yards of coordinating fabric for backing and binding

66" x 78" piece of batting*

3 yards of ¼"-diameter (or ⅛"-diameter) elastic cording

I recommend a single layer of 80/20 cotton/polyester blend batting or 100% cotton batting. For this project, 100% polyester batting is not recommended.

As quilters, we spend lots of time at the ironing board. I know I sure do. I've been making my own ironing board covers since I started free-motion quilting. I love using my favorite fabrics to brighten up my quilting space and make my pressing time a little more cheery. The cover that's on my board now was made from a special Kimono fabric given to me by my dear friend Makiko, who lives in Japan. In the cover shown, I've pieced together 5" charm squares, which gives lots of opportunity to practice print tracking. If the print in each square is different, you'll have the chance to stitch 79 different designs, just 5" at a time, all in one project.

INSTRUCTIONS

This layout minimizes the bulk created by the seams, which is preferred for a patchwork ironing-board cover.

1. Lay out the print squares in seven rows of five squares each and seven rows of six squares each as shown in the diagram following step 2. When you are pleased with the arrangement, sew the squares together into rows. Press the seam allowances open. Return each row to its original position in the layout.

2. Fold a five-square row in half to find the center of the row and finger-press to crease. Align the center seam on a six-square row with the crease and pin in place. Sew the rows together and press the seam allowances open. Join the remaining rows in the same way and press the seam allowances open. Sew the two remaining squares together. Press the seam allowances open and sew them to the five-square row on the end of the cover. The cover should measure 30½" x 75½".

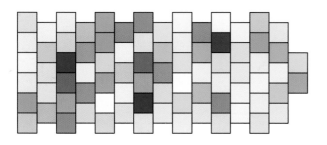

3. From the backing fabric, cut two 33" x 42" pieces. Join the pieces and press the seam allowances open. Trim the backing to measure 33" x 78".

4. Layer the cover with backing and batting. Baste using your preferred method.

5. Choose a few elements in each print to track. Quilting small bits on all the various squares will give you lots of experience in one quick project. If there is a print that you can't figure out how to track, just stipple through that square and move on to the next one.

6. Place your ironing board upside down on top of the quilted cover. Mark a line 3" from the edge of the ironing board, so that the cover is exactly 3" larger than the ironing board on all sides.

Make a Paper Pattern

You can put your ironing board on top of a length of freezer paper or doctor's office paper to make a paper pattern that can be reused time and time again.

7. Cut out the cover, cutting on the marked line. Fold the cover in half lengthwise to find the center on the bottom (wide) end. On both sides of the center crease, pin-mark ½" from the crease for the starting and ending points for the binding.

8. From the remaining backing fabric, cut six 2½" x 42" strips. Join the strips end to end using a diagonal seam as described on page 94. Press the strip in half lengthwise, wrong sides together. On one short end, fold over ¼" to the wrong side and then fold over ¼" again and press. Fold the strip lengthwise again. Starting at one of the pins with a backstitch, sew the binding to the cover. Stop stitching about 3" from the second pin. Trim the end of the binding ½" beyond the pin. Fold the end over in the same manner as before. Finish stitching the binding, ending with a backstitch.

9. Place the elastic cording inside the binding, next to the raw edge of the cover. Fold the binding over to the back of the cover. On the back, machine stitch the binding in place, being careful not to catch the elastic in the stitching. (You should be able to feel the elastic to easily avoid sewing over it.) Do not pull the elastic, just let it lie inside the casing.

10. With the cover wrong side up, place your ironing board upside down on top of the cover. Gently pull the elastic until it is taut. Adjust the cover as needed so that it fits snugly and is flat. Once the elastic is pulled as tightly as needed, tie the ends together in a bow. There's no need to worry about a fancy knot, as the stretch of the elastic will keep the bow tight, while still allowing you to remove the cover easily for washing.

Swirls

When I was still quite new to free-motion quilting, I had been making quilts for at least seven years, but I had never made one for myself. Since I had recently learned to quilt feathers, I decided it was time to piece a quilt top for myself—and be brave and stitch feathers across half of it! I was feeling quite proud about how the quilting turned out—even a bit cheeky—and wanted to show it to someone who would care. I had been following the career of Angela Walters and considered her quilting to be the best, so I emailed her pictures of my half-quilted quilt and asked her what design she thought I should use for the rest of the quilt.

To my amazement, she responded right away and was very encouraging about my quilting. She suggested I use swirls for the rest of the quilt. I was thrilled to have her expert advice, and she was right. Swirls worked perfectly for that quilt, and I always think of Angela whenever I quilt this design!

Swirls work well almost anywhere. You can manipulate the shape of a swirl by creating a half or even quarter swirl, or stitch around one swirl to create more layers of swirls to fill a space as needed. They're fun to stitch and pair well with many other designs. I find this is one of my most commonly used quilting designs because it is so very versatile and good looking.

INSTRUCTIONS

1. Set up your machine following "Five Prep Steps for Free-Motion Quilting" on page 21, and prepare a practice square.

2. Making sure your hands are in the proper position for maximum fabric control, sew five or six stitches in place before slowly stitching a large circle. When you are ½" from your starting point, stitch inward, staying about ½" inside the stitched line.

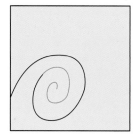

3. Continue stitching about ½" from the stitched line until you reach the center of the circle.

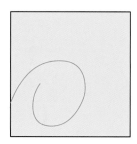

4. Stitching between the lines, stitch out of the circle until you reach the starting point.

5. Stitch another circle next to the first and then stitch another spiral. Continue stitching spirals to fill your practice square.

6. When you have only enough room to stitch half a spiral, stitch an arc to fill the space, and then stitch another arc ¼" inside the first. Continue filling the space with arcs ¼" apart until you have filled the area.

Vary the Size

You don't have to stop stitching your spiral right where you began it. You can quilt outer layers of increasingly large swirls. This as an easy way to fill more space, and the size variations will add to the visual interest of the design.

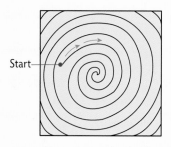

Start

Pieced and quilted by Molly Hanson

FINISHED SIZE

10" x 9" x 2" deep

MATERIALS

Yardage is based on 42"-wide fabric. Fat quarters measure 18" x 21".

½ yard of dark-turquoise solid for outer bag

1 fat quarter of medium-aqua solid for outer bag

1 fat quarter of light-aqua solid for outer bag

½ yard of fabric for lining

½ yard of fabric for backing

1 piece, 16" x 22", of fusible fleece

Continued on page 78

Tassels are so much fun and can add a unique look to all sorts of designs. I got a crash course in tassel making from my mom when one got stuck in a vacuum cleaner. We were guests in a friend's home and the tassel was sewn to the corner of a very expensive duvet. I started to panic, but mom calmly showed me how to put the tassel back together. It looked as good as new when she was finished. This handbag and the "Palm Springs Weekender Bag" on page 81, both feature a tassel. I hope you will find them as fun, easy, and addictive to make as I do.

Continued from page 77

2 pieces, 10½" x 12½", of heavyweight nonwoven fusible interfacing

1 piece, 5" x 8", of paper-backed fusible web

2 O rings, 1½" diameter, for strap

1 O ring, ½" diameter, for tassel

CUTTING

From the dark turquoise, cut:
1 strip, 4½" x 42"; crosscut into 4 strips, 4½" x 10½"
1 strip, 2½" x 42"; crosscut 3 strips, 2½" x 3" (set aside the remaining strip)
1 strip, 4" x 21"
1 strip, 1½" x 2"

From the medium aqua, cut:
2 strips, 1¾" x 21"; crosscut into 4 strips, 1¾" x 10½"
1 rectangle, 5" x 8"

From the light aqua, cut:
1 strip, 2½" x 21"; crosscut into 2 strips, 2½" x 10½"
1 rectangle, 5" x 8"
1 strip, 1" x 4"

From the lining fabric, cut:
2 rectangles, 10½" x 12½"
4 rectangles, 5" x 7"

From the backing fabric, cut:
2 rectangles, 12" x 14"

From the fusible fleece, cut:
2 rectangles, 10½" x 12½"
1 strip, 2½" x 21"

BAG BODY INSTRUCTIONS

1. Lay out the dark-turquoise, medium-aqua, and light-aqua strips as shown in the photo on page 77. Sew the strips together to make a rectangular unit. Press the seam allowances open. The unit should measure 12½" x 10½". Repeat to make a second identical unit.

2. Fuse a fleece rectangle to the wrong side of a unit from step 1. Spray baste a backing-fabric rectangle to the fleece side of the unit to make the bag front. Repeat the process to make the bag back.

3. Quilt the bag front and back as shown in the quilting map. You'll need to travel over previous stitching to get to the next swirl. Start in the

center and work your way outward. Trim the backing even with the bag front and the bag back.

Quilting map

4. Fuse a piece of interfacing to the wrong side of each lining rectangle.

5. With right sides together and using a ¼" seam allowance, sew two lining 5" x 7" rectangles together for a pocket, leaving a 3" opening on one of the 5" sides. Turn the rectangles right side out, taking care to push out the corners, and press. Turn the open seam allowances under; press. Topstitch along the edge. This will be the top edge of the pocket. Repeat to make a second pocket.

6. Center and pin both pockets to the right side of one lining rectangle, placing them ½" apart and 1" below the top edge. Topstitch around the side and bottom of each pocket, starting and stopping with a backstitch.

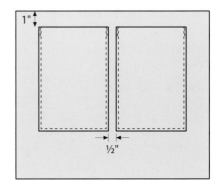

7. Place the lining rectangles right sides together and sew around the side and bottom edges.

8. To make box-pleat corners, mark 1" in and up from each bottom corner as shown. Cut out the square from each corner, cutting on the marked line. In one corner, place the side seam on top of the bottom seam. Pin the raw edges together. Sew the seam using a ¼" seam allowance. Box pleat the other corner in the same way.

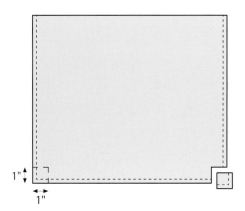

9. Repeat steps 7 and 8, sewing the bag front and back together, matching the seam intersections along the bottom edge, and making box-pleat corners. Turn the bag right side out.

10. To make the side tabs, press a dark-turquoise 2½" x 3" strip in half lengthwise, wrong sides together. Open the strip and fold both raw edges to the center crease; press. Fold the strip in half lengthwise again and press to make a ⅝" x 3" strip. Topstitch along both folded edges. Repeat to make a second tab.

11. Place the lining inside the bag, wrong sides together. Fold one tab in half and slip a 1½" O ring through the loop. Repeat with the other tab and O ring. On the exterior of the bag, pin a tab on top of each side seam.

TASSEL INSTRUCTIONS

1. To make the tassel tab, press the remaining dark-turquoise 2½" x 3" strip in half lengthwise, wrong sides together. Open the strip and fold both raw edges to the center crease; press. Fold both folded edges to the center crease and then fold the strip in half lengthwise again; press. The strip should now measure ⅜" x 3". Topstitch along both folded edges.

2. Apply a fusible-web rectangle to the wrong side of the medium-aqua 5" x 8" rectangle, following the manufacturer's instructions. Remove the paper backing and fuse the medium-aqua rectangle to the wrong side of the light-aqua 5" x 8" rectangle. On one long edge of the light-aqua rectangle, mark a line 2" from the edge. This will be the inside of the tassel.

3. Press the light-aqua 1" x 4" strip in half lengthwise, wrong sides together. Open the strip and fold both raw edges to the center crease. Fold the strip in half lengthwise again and press. Fold the strip in half with the raw edges aligned to make a loop. Slip the ½" O ring through the loop. Place the folded strip on the upper-left corner of the light-aqua rectangle and sew in place. Cut strips, ¼" apart, starting at the bottom of the rectangle and stopping at the marked line.

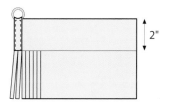

4. Starting with the left end, tightly roll the rectangle, making sure the ends are even. Hand stitch the tassel closed. On one short end of the dark-turquoise 1½" x 2" strip, fold over ¼" to the wrong side and press. Press the strip in half lengthwise, wrong sides together. Open the strip and fold both raw edges to the center crease. Starting with the raw edge, wrap the folded strip around the tassel, making sure the folded end of the strip covers the raw edges. Hand sew the folded edge of the strip in place to complete the tassel.

5. Thread the tassel tab through the O ring on the tassel. With the raw edges aligned, center the tab on the bag back and pin in place.

FINISHING

1. Press the remaining dark-turquoise 2½"-wide strip in half lengthwise, wrong sides together. On the top edge of the bag back, starting on one side seam and leaving a 7" tail, pin the strip to the exterior of the bag, making sure to align the raw edges and pin through the lining. Stop pinning at the other side seam.

2. Wrap both binding tails around the bag front and overlap them. Trim the strips so that they overlap exactly 2½". Sew the ends together as described in step 7 of "Binding" on page 94. Pin the binding to the bag front. Stitch in place. Fold the binding over the raw edges to the inside of the bag and pin in place, making sure to cover the line of stitches. On the bag front, stitch in the ditch next to the binding, making sure to stitch through the binding on the inside.

3. To make the strap, fuse the fleece 2½"-wide strip in the center of the dark-turquoise 4"-wide strip. Fold the long sides of the dark-turquoise strip over the fleece; press. Fold the strip in half lengthwise, wrong sides together, and press. Stitch ⅛" from both folded edges.

4. Slip one end of the strap through one of the O rings on the side of the bag. Fold the end up ½" toward the back of the strap. Sew in place, starting and stopping with a backstitch. Making sure the handle isn't twisted, repeat with the other end of the strap.

Palm Springs Weekender Bag

Pieced and quilted by Molly Hanson

FINISHED SIZE
16" x 13" x 6½" deep

MATERIALS
Yardage is based on 42"-wide fabric.

1 strip, 2½" x 42", *each of 10 assorted turquoise solids for outer bag*

¼ yard of dark-turquoise solid for strap and tab

¾ yard of fabric for bag lining

1 rectangle, 5" x 8", *each of 2 assorted turquoise solids for tassel*

¾ yard of 22"-wide fusible fleece for bag body and strap

2 D rings, 1¼" wide, for handles

Continued on page 82

Living in Palm Springs for 10 years, I still find myself constantly inspired by the beauty, both natural and man made, that surrounds me. From the epic blue skies to the swaying palm trees, gorgeous jagged mountains, and stark, serene desert—this is a beautiful place. I set out to create the perfect bag for a weekend in Palm Springs, but I think it might just be the perfect bag for a weekend away anywhere. The bag will hold a couple of outfits and a few pairs of shoes. It's so easy, you can make it in a day—I promise! You'll get a lot of quilting practice with this project, so roll those sleeves up and get started.

Continued from page 81

2 spring snap clips, 1¾" x 1¾", for handles

1 O ring, ½" wide for tassel

5" x 8" piece of fusible web

22" all-purpose polyester zipper to match 1 fabric

4"-long piece of ¼"-wide elastic

I used Robert Kaufman Kona Cotton in the following colors: Cyan, Turquoise, Lagoon, Robin Egg, Aqua, Capri, Breakers, Emerald, Glacier, and Everglade. For the strap and tabs, I used Cyan. For the tassel, I used one rectangle each of Capri and Aqua.

Recycled Hardware

I recycled the D rings and spring snap clips from a damaged bag I picked up at a thrift store for a few dollars. I highly recommend doing this if you can, because you'll find much nicer bag hardware than what is readily available in the purse-supply section at a typical craft store. Between my own closet, thrift stores, and the clearance departments at big-box retailers, I have found many bags I can recycle just for their hardware, and I've spent less than $5 each. You can't even buy boring sets of purse hardware at the craft store for under $5! Other great sources of bag hardware are luggage straps and D-ring belts.

CUTTING

From the lining fabric, cut:
2 pieces, 16" x 22"

From the dark-turquoise solid, cut:
1 strip, 6" x 22"*
2 rectangles, 3" x 6"
1 strip, 1½" x 2"

From the fusible fleece, cut:
2 pieces, 20" x 22"
1 strip, 4" x 20"*

Refer to "Perfect Strap Length" on page 84.

BAG BODY INSTRUCTIONS

1. Cut the 2½"-wide strips in half to make 20 strips, 2½" x 21". Arrange the strips into two identical stacks of 10 strips each. Lay out one stack of strips, arranging them from dark to light and back to dark as shown in the photo on page 81. Join the strips along their long edges to make a strip set. Press the seam allowances open. Use the remaining strips to make a second identical strip set.

2. Fuse a piece of fleece to the wrong side of each strip set. Spray baste a lining rectangle to the fleece side of the strip set to make the bag front. Repeat to make the bag back.

3. Quilt the bag front and back as shown in the quilting map. You'll need to travel over previous stitching to get to the next swirl.

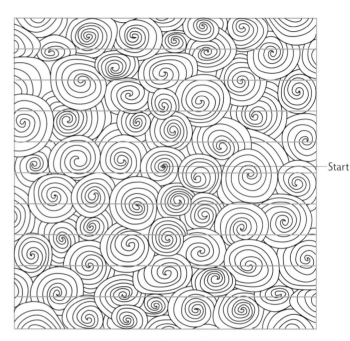
Start

Quilting map

4. Trim the lining even with the edges of the bag front. Zigzag stitch around the raw edges. Trim and zigzag stitch the bag back.

5. Referring to "Zippers" on page 93, sew the zipper to the top of the bag front and back, making sure the sides of the bag are aligned. Press and then topstitch ⅛" from the edge of the seam.

6. Unzip the zipper a little over halfway. You will be turning the bag right side out through the open zipper. With the lining side facing out, align the raw edges along the sides and bottom and pin in place, making sure to match the seam intersections on each side. Reduce the stitch length to ensure a strong, heavy-duty bag. Starting with a backstitch, sew around the side and bottom edges, stopping with a backstitch.

7. To make box-pleat corners, mark 3" in and up from each bottom corner as shown. Cut out the square from each corner, cutting on the marked line.

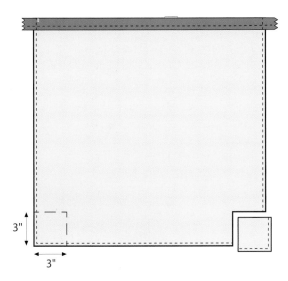

3"

3"

8. On one corner, place the bottom seam on top of the side seam. Pin the raw edges together. Reduce the stitch length and sew the seam using a ¼" seam allowance. Then zigzag stitch over the raw edges so they won't fray. Repeat to box pleat the other bottom corner.

9. Turn the bag right side out, pushing out the top and bottom corners.

STRAP AND TAB INSTRUCTIONS

1. To make a tab, press a dark-turquoise 3" x 6" strip in half lengthwise, wrong sides together. Open the strip and fold both raw edges to the center crease. Fold the strip in half lengthwise again and press. Fold the strip in half with the raw edges aligned to make a ¾" x 3" strip. Topstitch around all the edges, ⅛" away, to complete the tab. Repeat to make a second tab.

2. Fold one tab in half and slip a D ring through the loop. Sew across the tab, as close to the D ring as possible, starting and stopping with a backstitch. Repeat with the other tab and D ring.

3. On one top corner of the bag, place the zipper on top of the side seam. Separate the flaps on one tab and insert the corner of the bag between the flaps. Sew the tab in place; take your time and sew slowly. You may need to turn

the wheel with your hand to sew through all the layers. Repeat with the other tab and top corner of the bag.

4. To make the strap, fuse the 4"-wide strip of fleece in the center of the dark-turquoise 6"-wide strip. Fold the long sides of the dark-turquoise strip over the fleece; press. Fold the strip in half lengthwise, wrong sides together, and press. Stitch ⅛" from both folded edges. Using the edge of your presser foot as a guide, stitch straight lines ¼" apart through the middle of the strap.

5. Slip one end of the strap through a spring snap clip. Fold the end up ½" toward the back of the strap. Sew in place, starting and stopping with a backstitch. Repeat with the other end of the strap. Clip the strap onto the bag.

Perfect Strap Length

I cut a 4" x 20" strip of fusible fleece for my strap. However, I'm very petite and I didn't want my bag hanging so low that I would bump it with my legs. To determine the best length of strap for you, hold the bag up to your body approximately where the bag would be when you were carrying it. Have a friend measure from one of the top corners, over your shoulder and back down to the other corner. Keep in mind that the bag will hang 1" to 2" lower when it's full of stuff. Add 4" to that measurement and cut your batting strip to that length. Cut the fabric strip 2" longer than the batting strip.

TASSEL INSTRUCTIONS

1. Apply the fusible-web rectangle to the wrong side of a turquoise 5" x 8" rectangle, following the manufacturer's instructions. Remove the paper backing and fuse the rectangle to the wrong side of the remaining turquoise 5" x 8" rectangle. On one long edge of the lightest rectangle, mark a line 2" from the edge. This will be the inside of the tassel.

2. Fold the piece of elastic in half with the raw edges aligned to make a loop. Slip the ½" O ring through the loop. Place the elastic on the upper-left corner of the marked rectangle as shown in the diagram following step 3 on page 79. Sew in place. Cut strips, ¼" apart, starting at the bottom of the rectangle and stopping at the marked line.

3. Starting with the left end, tightly roll the rectangle, making sure the ends are even. Hand stitch the tassel closed. On one short end of the dark-turquoise 1½" x 2" strip, fold over ¼" to the wrong side and press. Press the strip in half lengthwise, wrong sides together. Open the strip and fold both raw edges to the center crease. Starting with the raw edge, wrap the folded strip around the tassel, making sure the folded end of the strip covers the raw edges. Hand sew the folded edge of the strip in place to complete the tassel.

4. Attach the tassel to the zipper pull.

Custom Quilting by Combining Designs

Congratulations, you have now learned all the quilting designs in this book. These designs have taught you the fundamentals of quilting and the most often-used, beginner-friendly quilting designs. The difference between quilting your project and *custom* quilting your project is in the clever combination of quilt designs. By thoughtfully combining one or more designs when quilting a block, or quilt, you can enhance the piecing by creating different textures. You can add visual interest to negative space, and can use your quilting to strengthen a theme in your quilt. For example, you can use pebble quilting to enhance a winter- or holiday-themed quilt by making a white background look like snow. Good design comes from practice and lots of trial and some error. Sketching is key to combining designs in a way that will maximize your quilting.

For the next project, you'll be planning your own design combinations in the center portion of each block in a quilt. To prepare, I recommend you start sketching designs in combination, getting as creative as you want. This is your chance to feature your skills, and these sketches will be a reminder of your beginning days of free-motion quilting. I'm calling this project "Art Gallery Quilt" because I want you to think of each frame as an opportunity to showcase a design combination you are proud of. You'll see my own design combinations on the sample quilt. I hope they inspire you and give you some ideas to experiment with. Please sketch and plan your own unique quilt, so you can gain the experience of combining designs and creating a quilting map.

INSTRUCTIONS

1. Fill several pages of your sketchbook with design combinations. When you have nine combinations that you like, practice drawing them again and see if there is anything you can do to make them better. When completely satisfied with the sketches for each block, it's time for the next step.

2. Make a practice sandwich for each block and practice quilting the designs as you have planned them. These practice squares can be saved and turned into a number of the projects in the book, especially the organizing bowls, place mats, and pillows—so be sure to make good use of them.

   You're now ready to move on to making your quilt. Piecing it will be elevated to a new level of fun, with the visions of your own custom quilting designs dancing through your head.

Wait, This Feels Different!

The time has come to quilt a real quilt. You'll notice that moving a large quilt while you're stitching it is different than quilting a smaller piece; the weight of the quilt makes it harder to move around freely. Getting used to the weight of a larger quilt can be a challenge, but these tips should help.

Divide your quilt into quarters. Quilting a large surface becomes much more manageable when you focus on one quarter at a time. Start in the center of the quadrant and work your way toward the outer corner, filling in the quadrant as you go. That way you can focus on moving and dealing with a manageable area of the quilt, no matter how big or small your machine is.

Pile your quilt around you. Don't roll the quilt to fit it into the throat of the machine, but rather "pile" it around you by loosely scrunching it to fit whatever area you need. Make sure you scrunch it enough to keep it from hanging off the front and back edges of the table as you quilt; the weight of the quilt hanging off the table will make it nearly impossible to move properly and will certainly fatigue your arms.

Take the time to stop and readjust. Quilting a large quilt can be easy and relaxing if you take the time to properly adjust the quilt around you for maximum success. This means stopping often to reposition the quilt and make sure it's not hanging off the table. If something feels different (such as it's harder to move the quilt), then the quilt probably needs to be adjusted.

Make sure you're comfortable, make sure your quilt is moving easily and freely, and take it one quadrant at a time. Then you'll be able to quilt even large quilts with ease!

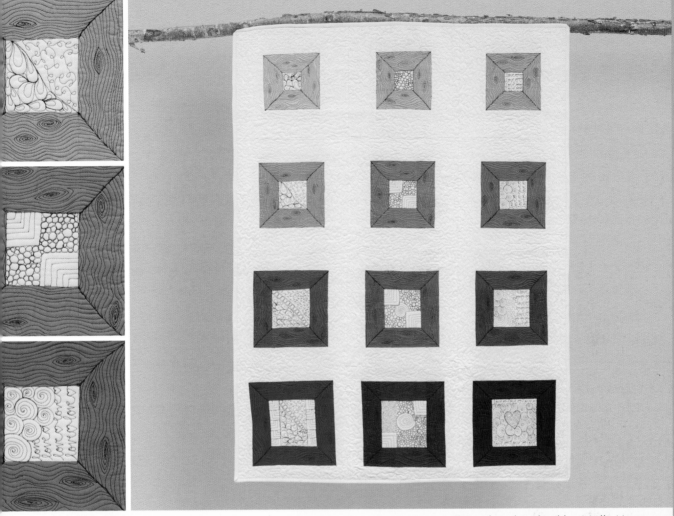

Pieced and quilted by Molly Hanson

FINISHED SIZE

Quilt: 36½" x 48½"
Blocks: 12" x 12"

MATERIALS

Yardage is based on 42"-wide fabric. A fat quarter measures 18" x 21".

1⅞ yards of ivory solid for blocks and binding

12 fat quarters or 10" squares of assorted shades of blue solids for blocks (3 light, 3 medium, 3 medium-dark, and 3 dark)

1⅜ yards of fabric for backing

38" x 44" piece of batting

Ivory and blue threads for quilting

Do you feel like a budding artist yet? You should! You've learned new skills and your designs have improved. You've tackled all sorts of techniques to make usable, functional, good-looking items for your life and home. If you don't quite feel like an artist yet, take a second to look over your achievements. This quilt is specifically designed to highlight your newly honed quilting skills. It's very simple and fast to make, and it's just the right size to start with. Notice how quilting can transform even a simple design like this one. Your new skills give you the ability to take any quilt to the next level: art-gallery worthy!

CUTTING

From the ivory solid, cut:
4 strips, 3½" x 42"; crosscut the strips into:
  6 rectangles, 3½" x 12½"
  6 rectangles, 3½" x 6½"
  3 squares, 3½" x 3½"
4 strips, 3" x 42"; crosscut the strips into:
  6 rectangles, 3" x 7½"
  6 rectangles, 3" x 12½"
9 strips, 2½" x 42"; crosscut 4 of the strips into:
  6 rectangles, 2½" x 8½"
  6 rectangles, 2½" x 12½"
  3 squares, 2½" x 2½"
4 strips, 2" x 42"; crosscut the strips into:
  6 rectangles, 2" x 9½"
  6 rectangles, 2" x 12½"
1 strip, 5½" x 42"; crosscut into 3 squares,
  5½" x 5½". Trim the remainder of the strip
  to 4½" wide and crosscut into 3 squares,
  4½" x 4½".

From each of the light-blue solids, cut:
2 squares, 2½" x 2½" (6 total)
2 rectangles, 2½" x 6½" (6 total)

From each of the medium-blue solids, cut:
2 rectangles, 2½" x 3½" (6 total)
2 rectangles, 2½" x 7½" (6 total)

From each of the medium-dark blue solids, cut:
2 rectangles, 2½" x 4½" (6 total)
2 rectangles, 2½" x 8½" (6 total)

From each of the dark-blue solids, cut:
2 rectangles, 2½" x 5½" (6 total)
2 rectangles, 2½" x 9½" (6 total)

PIECING THE BLOCKS

Keep all the blue pieces together by like fabric/shade.

1. Sew matching light-blue 2½" squares to opposite sides of an ivory 2½" square. Press the seam allowances open.

2. Sew matching light-blue 2½" x 6½" rectangles to the top and bottom of the unit from step 1. Press the seam allowances open.

3. Sew ivory 3½" x 6½" rectangles to opposite sides of the unit from step 2. Press the seam allowances open. Sew ivory 3½" x 12½" rectangles to the top and bottom of the unit. Press the seam allowances open. The block should measure 12½" x 12½".

4. Repeat steps 1–3 to make a total of three light-blue blocks for row 1.

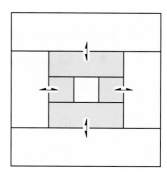

Make 3.

5. Sew matching medium-blue 2½" x 3½" rectangles to opposite sides of an ivory 3½" square. Press the seam allowances open.

6. Sew matching medium-blue 2½" x 7½" rectangles to the remaining sides of the ivory square. Press the seam allowances open.

7. Sew ivory 3" x 7½" rectangles to opposite sides of the unit from step 6. Press the seam allowances open. Sew ivory 3" x 12½" rectangles to the remaining sides of the unit. Press the seam allowances open.

8. Repeat steps 5–7 to make a total of three medium-blue blocks for row 2.

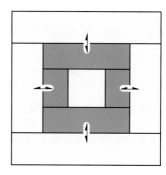

Make 3.

9. Repeat the process, using the ivory 4½" squares, the medium-dark blue 2½" x 4½" and 2½" x 8½" rectangles, and the ivory 2½" x 8½" and 2½" x 12½" rectangles to make three medium-dark blue blocks for row 3.

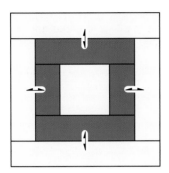

Make 3.

10. Repeat the process, using the ivory 5½" squares, the dark-blue 2½" x 5½" and 2½" x 9½" rectangles, and the ivory 2" x 9½" and 2" x 12½" rectangles to make three dark-blue blocks for row 4.

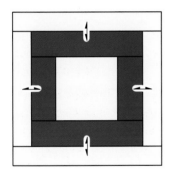

Make 3.

ASSEMBLING AND FINISHING THE QUILT

1. Lay out the blocks in four rows, with light-blue blocks in the top row, the medium-blue blocks in the second row, medium-dark blue blocks in the third row, and the dark-blue blocks in the bottom row. Sew the blocks together in rows. Press the seam allowances open.

2. Sew the rows together. Press the seam allowances open.

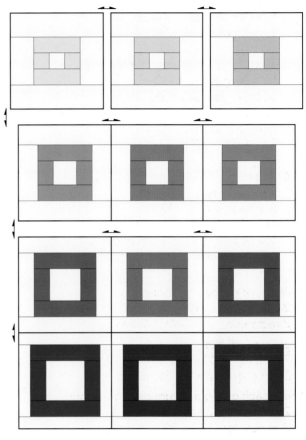

Quilt assembly

3. Layer the quilt top with backing and batting; pin baste the layers together. Refer to "Pin Basting" on page 14 as needed.

4. Referring to the quilting map for each row (page 90), quilt the blocks in the following order.

A: Stitch in the ditch around the center square.

B: Fill the block centers with your chosen designs.

C: Stitch from corner to corner in the blue rectangles to create a mitered corner look for your "frame."

D: Stitch in the ditch around the blue rectangles.

E: Fill the blue rectangles with wood-grain quilting, working from mitered edge to mitered edge on each side.

F: Fill the ivory rectangles with stippling as your background fill.

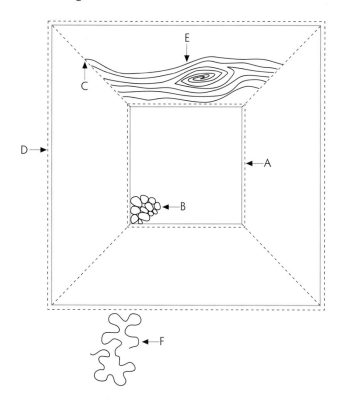

I encourage you to come up with your own plan or combination of designs for the center squares. Using a wood-grain design in the blue fabric will emphasize the frame appearance, and stippling in the background will make the quilt cohesive. In my quilt, I used dark-blue thread in the center blocks and frames, and ivory thread for the stippling so that it blended in.

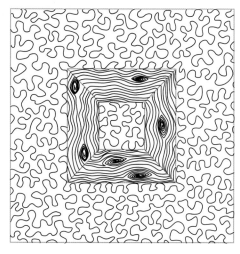

Row 1
Quilting map

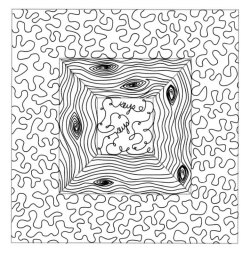

Row 2
Quilting map

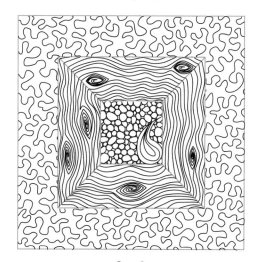

Row 3
Quilting map

Row 4
Quilting map

5. Trim away the excess batting and backing even with the quilt top. Referring to "Binding" on page 94, use the remaining ivory 2½"-wide strips to bind the edges.

Troubleshooting Guide

When facing problems with your quilting, whether it's a tension issue, a thread issue, or a horrific noise your machine is making, you'll find there's always one common element—stress! I have personally experienced every quilting atrocity one can think of. I have stitched huge sections of a quilt before realizing the backing was flipped up and a majority of the back wasn't covered. I have stitched with thread purchased at the same time and place, and same brand and color, only to find that one spool acts completely fine while the second gives me nothing but problems because it has gone bad and lost its strength. I have stitched through my index finger and embedded a portion of the needle inside my finger. Gross and painful! I can assure you, after surviving all of this and so much more, is that under absolutely no circumstances has freaking out ever helped me. But being calm, and methodical, and taking time to evaluate the problem and react accordingly helps *every single time*. So relax. Take a deep breath. Walk away for a few minutes if need be and revisit your problem with a calm, can-do attitude, and you too will survive your own quilting atrocities and live to tell about them!

TROUBLESHOOTING TENSION

Your tension is acting strangely, and you are either getting loose, sloppy-looking stitches on the top or bottom, or bird's nests on the bottom, or super-tight stitches that result in the bottom thread being pulled tight and visible on the top.

Rethread your machine first. Start over completely and rethread, making sure the thread slips through the tension disks in your machine.

Change out the bobbin for another. Wind a new bobbin if necessary. Don't use the same bobbin you were just using; try a completely different one. Occasionally when bobbins aren't wound correctly they cause tension problems while quilting. Sometimes bobbins can warp and not move properly inside the machine. Trying a new one will tell you if that is the problem.

Change your needle for a brand-new one. While doing so, take the time to clean out the dust and oil your machine.

Turn the sewing machine off. Leave it for a few hours or overnight. Sometimes machines get too hot when they have been running for a long time. Free-motion quilting puts more stress on your machine than normal sewing does, so this can accelerate the problem and affect your stitch quality. One of my machines can't be used for more than four hours before acting strangely, but often I sit at it the next day and have no problems.

Seek Professional Help

If you're still having problems, take your machine to a professional and have it evaluated. Most towns have a sewing-machine repair shop, and some may use the branding of a certain manufacturer, but don't let that deter you. Call and ask if they can service your machine. Often these shops repair and service all brands, even though they sell only one or two brands. A machine in good working order is essential for free-motion quilting, so proper maintenance is an absolute must.

THREAD TIPS

Your thread keeps breaking or fraying.

Rethread your machine. Make sure the thread is coming off the spool or cone the way your manual says it should. Don't partially rethread the machine—start completely over, and make sure the presser foot is in the up position or else the thread won't sink into the tension disks properly.

Change your needle. Sometimes needles have tiny burrs that you can't see with the naked eye, but in the right spot a burr can wreak havoc on thread. A new needle will fix the problem right away if a burr is the culprit.

Try a new cone or spool of thread. Thread will go bad over time. When that happens, breaking and shredding are the mess that gets left behind. Reasons for thread going bad range from humidity and heat issues, to the age of the thread. Plus, you really never know when you buy a spool of thread just how old it is, or how it has been stored. This can be frustrating. I haven't had many problems with bad thread, but when it has happened, and I have had to toss out a whole cone of thread, it always bums me out. Chalk it up as part of the price we pay to play, I guess. If nothing else helps, it's probably bad thread. Toss it out and go for another spool.

A Few Basic Sewing Tips

In preparing this book, my goal was to provide very simple projects that won't take a long time to make, so you can focus your time and energy on the quilting process. But although these projects are quick, they teach important techniques—different ways I have come up with over the years to use my quilted practice squares and samples. I will explain some of these techniques here for reference.

ROTARY CUTTING

I recommend rotary cutting for all my projects. From trimming and squaring up quilts before binding them to cutting out patchwork squares, there is no better way to cut fabric for quilting. I recommend a cutting mat as large as you can accommodate, a 24"-long clear acrylic ruler, and a 12½" square ruler.

Position a long ruler along the right edge of the fabric, with a horizontal line on your ruler aligned with the fold and the right cutting edge just inside all the layers of the fabric. Cut along the long, right edge of the ruler. Discard the fabric slivers.

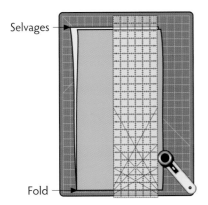

Align a horizontal mark on the ruler with the fold. Cut along the edge of the ruler.

To cut a strip, place the long ruler so it overlaps the fabric, aligning the marking for the desired width even with the cut (left) edge of the fabric. For example, to cut a 2½"-wide strip, place the 2½" line

on the ruler along the clean-cut edge of the fabric. (Reverse the directions if you are left-handed.)

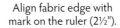
Align fabric edge with mark on the ruler (2½").

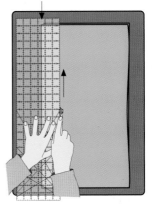

QUARTER-INCH SEAM ALLOWANCE

All of the projects use a ¼" seam allowance unless otherwise noted. I recommend using a ¼" patchwork foot for accurate piecing.

ZIPPERS

Some of my projects use zippers. If you've never installed a zipper before, don't worry. If done properly, it is both easy and addictive! If you are new to zippers, or have struggled with them in the past, I recommend hand or machine basting close to the seam edge so your zipper won't shift while sewing—this simple step practically guarantees success.

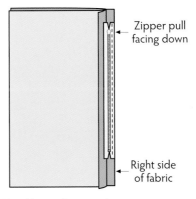
Zipper pull facing down

Right side of fabric

Hand baste close to edge.

If you want to baste by machine, set your stitch length as long as it will go. Using a zipper foot, stitch close to the edge of the zipper tape (away from the teeth). Then carefully sew as close to the teeth as possible, keeping the zipper lined up as you go. When you get to the zipper pull, stop with your needle down in the fabric and raise the presser foot. Making sure to leave your foot off the pedal of the machine to avoid any accidents, carefully wiggle the zipper pull out of the way so you can continue stitching unobstructed. Flip the zipper over, press toward the fabric, and topstitch ⅛" from the seam.

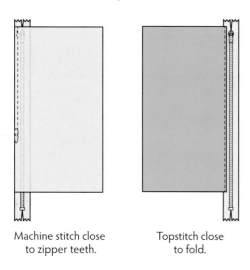

Machine stitch close to zipper teeth.

Topstitch close to fold.

BINDING

Finishing your project with a beautiful binding really adds that professional touch to your work. With that said, I must admit that I hate sewing on binding by hand. I know, it's terrible, I will spend weeks quilting something only to rush through the binding! Oh well, I am sure I'm not the only quiltmaker too busy to hand sew my binding. If you're like me and would like to know how I save lots of time, read on!

1. Cut the number of strips in the designated width as instructed in the project. Place the strips right sides together at right angles, with the bottom strip exactly ¼" below the top edge and ¼" to the right of the right edge of the top strip. Pin in place to secure.

2. Sew from corner to corner as shown. Trim the excess fabric, leaving a ¼" seam allowance. Continue sewing the strips together in the same manner until you have one long strip.

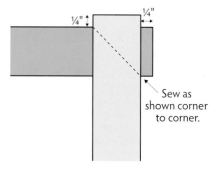

Sew as shown corner to corner.

3. Carefully fold the strip in half lengthwise, with wrong sides together, and press. Take your time, keeping the edges lined up and the crease nice and sharp. I wrap the binding around an empty spool of thread to prevent it from tangling while I'm sewing it to the quilt.

4. Starting at the middle on one side and aligning the raw edges, place one end of the binding strip on the right side of the quilt. Leaving an 8" to 10" tail, sew the binding using a ¼" seam allowance. Stop stitching ¼" from the corner, and backstitch one or two stitches. Clip the thread and remove the quilt from the machine.

5. Turn the quilt to prepare for sewing the next edge. Fold the binding up away from the quilt so that the fold forms a 45° angle as shown. Then fold it back down onto itself, even with the raw edge of the quilt. The fold should be aligned with the corner of the quilt. Starting at the fold, sew the binding to the next side of the quilt in the same way, stopping ¼" from

the corner. Fold the next miter and continue, stitching each side and mitering the corners as you go.

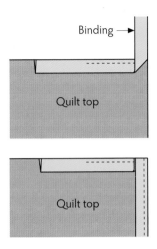
Binding →

Quilt top

Quilt top

6. Stop stitching about 10" from the starting point and remove the quilt from the machine. Lay the quilt edge flat and overlap the beginning and ending tails. Trim the tails perpendicular to the quilt edge so that the amount of overlap exactly matches the width of your binding strips. For example, if you started with 2½"-wide binding strips, overlap the strips by 2½".

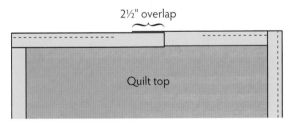
2½" overlap

Quilt top

Overlap binding ends and trim.

7. Unfold the binding strips and place them right sides together, overlapping them at right angles as shown. Draw a line from corner to corner on the wrong side of one binding strip and pin before stitching. Stitch along the drawn line. Check that your binding is just the right length for the quilt, and then trim the excess fabric, leaving a ¼" seam allowance.

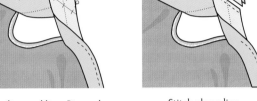
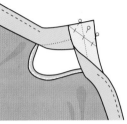

Draw diagonal line. Pin ends together, matching corners.

Stitch along line and trim excess.

8. On the quilt front, press the binding up, away from the quilt. Then wrap the binding over the edges of the quilt, with the folded edge covering the row of machine stitching, and press again. Use binding clips to hold the binding in place. At your sewing machine, with the quilt right side up, place the needle in the seam between the quilt and binding. Carefully and slowly stitch in the ditch, stopping to remove binding clips before you get to them and making sure the back of the binding is caught in the stitching. If you used 2½"-wide strips and a ¼" seam allowance to attach the binding, you should have plenty of fabric to wrap around the back and stitch. If you like, you can use a decorative stitch instead of stitching in the ditch. This will make it even easier to catch the binding on the back, since decorative stitches are wider. They also add a nice touch!

About the Author

From the time Molly Hanson was very young, creativity has been her constant companion. Throughout her life, she has sought and embraced any way she could find to express her ideas. When she made her first quilt, Molly found an unrivaled outlet for her creativity, and she was hooked. She loves the whole process, especially coming up with her own designs, and is well known for being fearless in her quilting adventures. She truly is not afraid to make a mistake, or even fail. She loves trying new things.

When Molly tried free-motion quilting, her head began to swirl with all the possibilities of adding this extra layer of art to her quilts. She loved the control that she gained over the artistic process by being able to quilt her own quilts. She was officially hooked. For a year, Molly spent every spare second she had quilting and sketching her quilting designs. With hours and hours of practice she saw quick improvement and enjoyed turning some of the ideas swirling through her head into reality.

Since then, she has quilted for customers including fabric companies, authors, bloggers, and pattern companies. Her other accomplishments include a pattern featured in a magazine; her work featured in videos and advertising for a fabric company; quilted projects published in a book; and she has designed and quilted quilts in major shows. For Molly, the highlight of it all has been writing this book. She hopes to inspire others to join her in the ability to quilt their own quilts, and have control of their process and how it all turns out from start to finish. You can read more about her quilting adventures at SewWrongSewRight.blogspot.com.

Acknowledgments

I would like to thank Angela Walters and Karen Burns for seeing something in me and championing me. I can't tell you how much your support and love have helped and encouraged me.

And thanks to my readers. I hope I inspire you to try something new, to be a bit fearless, to make something you've never made before, and to become a free-motion quilter. Thank you for buying and reading my book!